Contents

LIVERPOOL
JOHN MOORES UNIVERSITY
AVRIL ROBARTS LRC
TITHEBARN STREET
LIVERPOOL L2 2ER
TEL. 0151 231 4022

1.   Community mediation services: criteria for accepting cases.

2a.   Council A, Area 'a': table showing how hourly salary and related costs were calculated for Council A, area 'a'; based on actual case records and also based on time records derived from monitoring exercise in two neighbouring areas.

2b.   Council A, area 'a': table showing case costs according to outcome.

3.   Council A, Area 'b': sample chart showing how costs were calculated for one of the case histories referred to in the text (case 12: cumulative times and costs to housing).

4.   Council A, Environmental Health Department: tables showing how costs were calculated.

5.   Sandwell Mediation Service: series of tables showing how costs were calculated. Table 5c shows the unit costs calculated on the same basis as for Council A's housing and environmental health departments.

6.   Derby Mediation Service: tables showing how unit costs were calculated using the same approach as for Sandwell and also the housing and environmental service departments in Council A.

Neighbour Disputes

Comparing the cost-effectiveness of mediation and alternative approaches

WITHDRAWN

LIVERPOOL
JOHN MOORES UNIVERSITY
AVRIL ROBARTS LRC
TITHEBARN STREET
LIVERPOOL L2 2ER
TEL. 0151 231 4022

LIVERPOOL JMU LIBRARY

3 1111 00793 4563

Centre for Criminological
and Legal Research
The University of Sheffield

October 1996

Jim Dignan,
Angela Sorsby and
Jeremy Hibbert

Neighbour Disputes: Comparing the cost-effectiveness of mediation with alternative approaches
by Jim Dignan, Angela Sorsby and Jermey Hibbert

First published in Great Britain in 1996 by
the Centre for Criminological and Legal Research, University of Sheffield

Copyright © 1996 the authors

All rights reserved. No part of this publication may be reproduced,
stored in a retrieval system, or transmitted, in any form or by any means,
electronic, mechanical, photocopying, recording or otherwise, without
the prior permission of the authors.

Designed and typeset by BBR, Sheffield,
and printed in the UK by H. Cave & Co., Leicester.

ISBN 1-872998-36-4

Centre for Criminological and Legal Research,
The University of Sheffield,
Conduit Road,
Sheffield S10 1FL

LIVERPOOL JOHN MOORES UNIVERSITY
LEARNING SERVICES

Accession No
06344 03/98

Class No
347.09 DIG

Aldham Robarts
0151-231-3701

I M Marsh
0151-231-5216

Foreword

In recent years, the number of neighbour disputes has escalated to become a significant problem not only in most towns and cities, but also in many rural areas. The media have highlighted some of the more extreme conflicts which cause misery and distress to those involved, and have on occasion led to violence, including murder.

Many local authorities have found their officers spending increasing and disproportionate amounts of time on these problems, and are therefore eager to find more effective ways of handling such disputes.

Neighbour mediation services originated in the 1980s, primarily as a response to the rising number of seemingly intractable neighbour disputes. Several of these initiatives were started by people in their own local communities and were found to be very effective. **MEDIATION UK** was formed in 1984 to bring together such initiatives and to help more new mediation services to come into existence. In the 1990s, the rate at which new services were being started began to accelerate as an increasing number of individuals, local authorities and other interested parties became aware of mediation, and as Environmental Health and Housing Departments began to develop strategic approaches to neighbour problems.

Those who were already enthusiastic about mediation felt that it was self-evident that the process was not only an important way of resolving disputes, but that it also saved money, particularly in comparison to the cases regularly reported in the media where initially minor neighbour disputes had escalated to the extent that they ended up costing thousands of pounds in court costs and legal fees. However, many in Central and Local Government, who were concerned that mediation would be just another 'add-on cost', required hard evidence to show that mediation really could save money.

These concerns were reflected in the funding problems experienced by mediation services.

Although a major effort was needed to start a neighbour mediation service, funding was relatively easy to find for the initial stages, usually from special local or national funding, for example crime prevention initiatives. However, as the new neighbour mediation services became established and began to bring tangible benefits to the local community, it was often found that the funding dried up. Such services were no longer considered to be 'innovative initiatives' and neither local authorities nor charities felt able to take over responsibility for funding.

MEDIATION UK felt it was vital to research the area of cost-effectiveness, at the same time as Central Government also began to take greater interest in neighbour mediation. We are grateful to the Lankelly Foundation, which funded the first stage of the research, including the survey of neighbour mediation services and the development of a system for collecting national statistics as a means to compile a full picture of mediation activity. We would like to thank the Department of the Environment for funding the cost-effectiveness research, which is the subject of this report.

MEDIATION UK set up a Research Steering Committee, including researchers, mediation practitioners and representatives from the Department of the Environment to oversee our work. Our thanks go to Bridged Canavan, Marian Liebmann, Tony Marshall, Peter Raynor (**MEDIATION UK**), Phil Clapp, Steve Guyon and David Riley (Department of the Environment) for all their valuable time and expertise.

The research was carried out by the Sheffield University team of Jim Dignan, Angela Sorsby and Jeremy Hibbert, who have wide experience of similar work. They have worked extremely hard and effectively over the period of this research and have produced a very readable and accessible report.

The report's findings show that there is genuine scope in some cases for significant savings to be made using mediation. Mediation will offer a more constructive solution for parties who are willing to give it a try, even in respect of some of the more intractable neighbour disputes that housing and environmental health departments have to deal with.

The findings provide a real advance in what is known about neighbour disputes and their costs. As with much research, however, the results expose gaps in our knowledge, and **MEDIATION UK** is keen to continue this work, subject to the availability of further funding.

Local authority managers, researchers, practitioners and anyone interested in developing more constructive ways of handling conflict will, we believe, find much in this report to influence their future practice.

Carey Haslam
Chair
MEDIATION UK

MEDIATION UK
and its member services

MEDIATION UK is a network of projects, organisations and individuals interested in mediation and other forms of constructive conflict resolution. It is a registered charity supported by grants and donations. **MEDIATION UK** is the only umbrella organisation for all initiatives and individuals interested in conflict resolution in the UK.

Currently it has a membership of 450, of which 150 are organisations and 300 are individuals. 110 of the organisations are mediation services:

Community/Neighbourhood mediation	75
Victim/Offender mediation	25
Conflict resolution work in schools	20

This adds up to more than 110 because some services do more than one kind of work.

Mediation – a definition

Mediation is a process whereby an impartial third party helps two disputing parties to sort out their disagreement. The parties, not the mediator, decide the terms of the agreement.

Community mediation services

The fastest growing area of work is in community and neighbourhood mediation. The community mediation services are spread throughout the UK.

Almost all use trained volunteers to do the mediation, and volunteers work in pairs, for safety and for maximum effect and learning. Most services have a paid coordinator, but a few run entirely on volunteers. Some cover large districts while others concentrate in a more pro-active way on small troublesome housing estates.

How a community mediation service operates

Most community mediation services take referrals from community agencies and disputants themselves. Mediators visit the first party (who has requested help) and then if appropriate, contact the second party, and visit if welcomed. If both parties wish, the case proceeds to mediation. Sometimes just listening to the parties helps them to solve their dispute on their own. Of the 30% that result in face-to-face mediation, about 80% result in agreements which hold over several months. Many agreements are also reached by 'shuttle mediation', with mediators acting as go-betweens for parties who do not actually meet. The mediators often follow up both parties after three months or so.

The most common complaints from neighbours are about noise (60%). The noise can be from music, hi-fi, DIY, dogs, children, TV, talking or household appliances. Other disputes concern boundaries, children, rubbish harassment, abuse and other annoyances.

Schools work

Some member projects specialise in schools work, and some community mediation services develop a 'schools group'. They go into schools and teach children how to resolve conflict in non-violent ways. Several of these projects are now also training children to be peer mediators for playground quarrels. There is increasing interest in this work, especially in its potential to reduce bullying.

Victim/offender work

These projects bring victims and offenders together to discuss the criminal offence that has occurred, to help mutual understanding and see if appropriate reparation can take place, e.g. paying the costs of damage, mending a wall, and/or an apology. These services may operate at the pre-court, court or post-sentence stage. The Alternatives to Violence Project (AVP) works in prisons to teach non-violent conflict resolution.

Other projects

There are many other interesting member projects, such as those developing conflict resolution through drama, or doing prejudice reduction work. They are all concerned with helping people to resolve conflicts in a constructive way.

For further information contact:

Tony Billinghurst
Director
MEDIATION UK
82a Gloucester Road
Bishopston
Bristol BS7 8BN

Tel: 0117 924 1234
Fax: 0117 944 1387

Acknowledgements

This research was funded by the Department of the Environment and the Lankelly Foundation. The project was conducted under the guidance of a Steering Committee made up of representatives from the Department of the Environment, the Home Office, Mediation UK, academics and co-ordinators of community-based mediation services. We wish to record our appreciation to all members of that committee for the helpful and constructive support and advice they provided throughout the course of the fieldwork, and also in the production of the four interim reports and this final report.

We are indebted to the many co-ordinators of Community Mediation Services who responded so helpfully to our general questionnaire survey, and in particular to Carole Cowell of Sandwell Mediation Service, Jackie Bates at Derby Mediation Service and Susan Parry at Bolton Neighbour Dispute Service.

We also owe a sincere debt of gratitude to the many people working in housing, legal and adminis-tration and environmental services in the local authority areas we selected as case studies. Because we are bound by undertakings of confidentiality we regret that we cannot publicly acknowledge their invaluable assistance and support, or even indicate their whereabouts. However, we do wish to put on record our deep appreciation for the way they generously committed their time and expertise to answering our queries.

Finally, we should also acknowledge the constant support and assistance we have received from Marian Liebmann, Margaret Woodward and the other staff at Mediation UK headquarters in Bristol.

JIM DIGNAN
ANGELA SORSBY
JEREMY HIBBERT

Preface

Disputes between neighbours have featured prominently in the media over the last few years, and many accounts have highlighted the shortcomings of existing legal procedures for dealing with them. This in turn has given added urgency to the quest for cheaper, quicker and more effective ways of dealing with the problems they pose, both for the disputants themselves and also the authorities that are called upon to deal with them.

The process of mediation offers an alternative to the more traditional legal and administrative approaches that have been found wanting in the past, and over the last decade there has been a rapid expansion in the number of community mediation projects providing such a service. Until now, however, no attempt has been made to evaluate the performance of mediation compared with other ways of dealing with neighbour disputes. Indeed, relatively little is known about the number and nature of neighbour disputes in Britain; their effects on those involved; the way they are dealt with; or their resource implications for the relevant agencies and for the community in general.

In 1994 the Department of the Environment and the Lankelly Foundation agreed to jointly fund a research project commissioned by Mediation UK which is a national umbrella organisation for various types of mediation initiatives in the United Kingdom, and the only one representing community mediation projects. The research specification for the project comprised a number of inter-related elements, the most important of which are set out below:

- To provide an up-to-date overview of the work of existing mediation services including rates and types of referral, numbers of cases dealt with in different ways and input and outcome measures including costs.

- To devise a standard data-collection system that would enable the above information to be regularly up-dated. [This aspect of the project was written up separately as an interim report (Dignan and Sorsby, 1995) and does not form part of the final report].

- To provide an up-to-date overview of the work of local authority housing and environmental health service departments in relation to neighbour disputes including case-loads and costs (including human and social costs as well as purely financial ones) of current procedures, potential scope for mediation etc.

- To work with a small number of case study mediation services and housing service departments to develop a method for reliably comparing costs and outcomes between very different types of procedures.

- To apply the above methodology to the latest available financial and case record data to enable reliable comparisons to be made, and conclusions to be drawn, about the effectiveness of mediation in relation to alternative ways of handing neighbour disputes.

- To consider the policy implications associated with the above findings, including the possible effects on demand of offering more mediation services (together with the cost implications), and the scale of services required in order to produce effective savings.

Work on the research project began in 1995 with a nation-wide questionnaire survey of the 34 community mediation services in existence at that time. Completed replies were received from 29 services which is equivalent to a response rate of 85.3%. Questionnaires were also sent to a further eleven services that had been identified by Mediation UK as 'soon to become operational'. Only two of the latter responded, though their returns were also included in the analysis.

A second nation-wide questionnaire survey was addressed to the relevant housing and environmental health service departments in a total of 57 local authorities (roughly one in seven of all local authorities in England and Wales).

Two distinct groups of authorities were selected for inclusion in the survey: those in areas served by a local community mediation service; and those in areas where no such service was available. The first group, which we refer to as 'Sample A', consisted of the relevant local authority for each of the 29 community mediation services taking part in the first survey referred to above. We then attempted to identify for each of these a broadly comparable council (in terms of type of council, population size, approximate geographical location and level of poll tax levied) in an area that lacked a local community mediation service. This yielded a second group of 28 councils which we refer to as 'Sample B'.

environmental services. However, in the remaining seven councils (four in sample A and three in sample B), the two sets of services were combined.[1]

Just under half the questionnaires were returned (46%) altogether. The response rate was slightly higher for Environmental Health Service departments (48%) than for Housing Departments (42%). The response rate was also slightly higher in the case of Sample A departments than for those in Sample B. Although the response rate was lower than we were hoping for, all the main council types were represented among those returning questionnaires, as can be seen from Table P.1.

Finally, we undertook a number of much more detailed case studies in respect of a small number of community mediation services and local authority housing and environmental service departments in order to collect additional information relating mainly to costs, case histories, inputs and outcomes.

For this part of the project we worked closely with four contrasting community mediation services, three local authority Housing Departments and one large Environmental Services department. The community mediation services are identified and described on page 75 of the report. Because of strong concerns expressed by Housing Service Directors and council solicitors over the sensitivity of the financial information we were requesting, the names and locations of the departments concerned are not disclosed in this report.[2]

In presenting our findings we will refer to a number of case histories. Some are based on newspaper reports, but most of them were compiled with the assistance of information which we obtained from the relevant case files. The case histories are intended to serve a number of purposes.

First, we have used them to illustrate the range and scale of costs (human, social and financial) that might be incurred by those who are involved in, or responsible for dealing with neighbour disputes. Where appropriate, we have obtained additional financial information from the relevant finance officers in our three case study councils.

Table P.1: Composition of questionnaire returns by type of council and department.

Sample A councils

Council type	Housing Services	Environmental Services	Combined Dept	Total
District Council	7	8	1	16
Metropolitan District Council	1	2	2	5
London Borough Council	3	3	0	6
Total	11	13	3	27

Sample B councils

Council type	Housing Services	Environmental Services	Combined Dept	Total
District Council	6	4	1	11
Metropolitan District Council	2	3	0	5
London Borough Council	2	4	0	6
Total	10	11	1	22

Because neighbour disputes pose rather different sets of problems for local authorities in their capacity as social landlords, and as enforcers of environmental health legislation, two distinct versions of the questionnaire were produced and sent to the relevant departments. In 50 of the local authorities there were separate departments for housing and

Secondly, we have also selected our case histories with a view to exploring the scope for (and limits of) mediation as a method of resolving neighbour disputes, and to highlight some of the policy issues that are involved. These are issues we will discuss more fully in Chapter 10 of the report.

We have numbered the case histories sequentially throughout the report since this should make it easier to identify them for discussion purposes, even though they have been derived from a variety of sources and will be used to illustrate a number of different themes.

We also refer in the report to a small number of sub-studies which we undertook in order to investigate specific issues, mainly in relation to the costs incurred by housing departments. These have been written up as case studies 1-3 and are all contained in Chapter 6 of the report.

Notes

1 These councils were sent both versions of the questionnaire. Of the four returns we received from combined departments, three councils returned the 'housing' questionnaire, and one the 'environmental services questionnaire.

2 Such was the concern over the sensitivity of the data we were requesting that our choice of council was inevitably dictated more by the willingness of individual councils to co-operate in this part of the survey than by geographical or methodological considerations.

LIVERPO.   ...SITY
LEARNING SERVICES

Summary of the Report

Neighbour disputes

Neighbours may come into conflict over an infinitely wide range of issues, and the form of that conflict is equally variable in terms of its duration and intensity. The behaviour complained of may range from merely inconsiderate or anti-social conduct to harassment, violent assaults and other forms of criminal activity such as drug-dealing.

Neighbour disputes are also commonplace. The present study suggests that the number of neighbour nuisance complaints reported each year to local authority housing and environmental health service departments could be upwards of 250,000, about two thirds of which are likely to be noise-related. However, it is known that the great majority of neighbour nuisance complaints are not reported to any of the agencies concerned with the problem. And, with the exception of noise complaints, very little is known abut the types of complaints involved, the way they are dealt with or their resource implications.

The research

One of the aims of the present study was to identify the range of costs incurred both by those embroiled in neighbour disputes and those with responsibility for handling them, and to seek to quantify these where possible. However, the main aim was to investigate the cost effectiveness of mediation compared with conventional methods of dealing with neighbour disputes.

The biggest challenge we faced was how to devise a method of comparing these approaches since they differ fundamentally in terms of their aims, methods, the context in which they operate and also their outcomes. In responding to this challenge we have sought to combine some of the quantitative techniques associated with conventional cost benefit analysis where appropriate, with a more qualitative approach that is sensitive to their limitations.

The report is based on the findings of two national surveys focusing on community mediation services and local authority health and environmental health departments, together with the findings of a series of much more detailed case studies involving both sets of agencies.

Measuring the impact of neighbour disputes

Neighbour disputes feature regularly in the media, and are often used to portray the quirkier side of human nature. However, there is also a darker side, since the effects on those involved can often be devastating. During the six year period up to December 1994 there were seventeen documented fatalities associated with neighbourhood noise complaints, and a newspaper content analysis conducted as part of the present study produced four reports of fatalities resulting from disputes between neighbours during the first eight months of 1996 alone. At a more mundane level, neighbour disputes can blight the lives of those involved for years on end and the report features a number of case histories illustrating the problem.

How neighbour disputes are dealt with

Most neighbour disputes are either ignored or dealt with informally by those affected. Only a minority are reported to the various agencies whose assistance is likely to be sought: principally local authority housing and environmental health departments and also the police. They in turn tend to deal informally with the great majority of complaints they receive, and only invoke their extensive legal powers in exceptional circumstances. This is partly because of the expense associated with their use, and partly because of limitations inherent in the nature of the remedies themselves, both of which we address in the report.

An alternative approach that has been developed over the last few years involves the use of mediation, which seeks to deal more constructively with the problem by enabling people to negotiate a mutually acceptable outcome with the help of a neutral third party. The report examines the role of community mediation services in relation to neighbour disputes and compares the approach used with conventional ways of dealing with the problem.

Resource implications for housing and environmental services

An important aim of the research has been to identify, and where possible to quantify, the full range of costs that might be incurred by two of the main agencies whose responsibilities encompass neighbour disputes. Prior to the research little was known of the resource costs to the agencies themselves.

The report's findings suggest that the amount of time that is devoted to tasks specifically relating to handling of neighbour disputes is much smaller than is commonly supposed, and that this largely reflects[1] the relatively limited input that is made in the great majority of cases. However, in a minority of cases involving informal intervention on the part of housing officers, and whenever more formal measures are invoked (including various forms of legal action and the rehousing of tenants) the costs involved are normally considerable and appear to offer genuine scope for significant savings to be made by using mediation in appropriate cases. The report's findings also call into question the effectiveness of both the formal and informal approaches conventionally adopted for neighbour disputes, and suggest that mediation may offer a more constructive solution where the parties are willing to give it a try.

Policy implications

Mediation can be an effective and cheaper way of dealing with neighbour disputes and a response which can help prevent disputes from escalating into more serious problems. The case for making greater use of mediation in the context of neighbour disputes is not founded on financial considerations alone so much as its claim to offer a potentially more constructive way of resolving a category of disputes that has not proved amenable to conventional forms of dispute resolution. Nevertheless, the report suggests that, provided it is properly targeted, mediation appears to offer scope for significant savings to be made in respect of some of the more intractable neighbour disputes that housing and environmental health departments are called upon to deal with.

The report proposes a strategy for increasing the number of cases that could successfully be resolved by means of mediation and identifies a number of suggestions for further research.

Note

1 An additional factor, as we shall see, may be the technique we relied on for assessing the amount of time devoted to a case. This involved the identification of all the specific actions taken in relation to a case, for which time estimates were sought. However, this does not take into account time that is not specifically allocated to any particular action but which might properly be attributable to a neighbour dispute case; for example time devoted to informal consultation or report writing. To this extent the times we recorded are likely to be conservative estimates.

1

Researching neighbour disputes: problems and pitfalls

Undertaking research into neighbour disputes and the way they are dealt with presents a number of problems which we will deal with under the following headings:

- definitional problems;

- data collection problems; and

- methodological problems

Definitional problems

Who is my neighbour? What is a neighbour dispute? In neither case is the definition entirely straight-forward.

For research purposes it seems sensible to define 'neighbours' as all those living within a particular locality or district, which would include not only the owners and occupiers of nearby premises but also their households and visitors. However, a much narrower and more legalistic definition is likely to be adopted by some of those responsible for dealing with disputes between neighbours, particularly local authority housing departments.[1] For example, complaints by owner occupiers against tenants, or indeed complaints by tenants against neighbouring owner occupiers are somewhat grey areas (Aldbourne Associates, 1993), regarding which local policies may well differ as to whether such complaints are recorded or processed. This has obvious implications for those seeking to investigate the scale of the problem and the way it is dealt with.

What is a neighbour dispute? Unlike crime, 'neighbour dispute' is not a legally defined category. Neighbours may come into conflict over an infinitely variable range of issues, and the form of that conflict is equally variable in terms of its duration and intensity. Thus, the behaviour complained of may range from merely inconsiderate or anti-social conduct to harassment, violent assaults and other forms of criminal activity such as drug-dealing. This in turn may

provoke a variety of responses from doing nothing to raising the matter with various authorities or even resorting to 'self-help', including the threat or use of serious violence.

Nor is it possible to agree on objective standards of what is 'reasonable' or 'unreasonable' behaviour since much will depend on factors such as the time of day, the nature, suitability and condition of the accommodation in question, as well as the relative ages, life-styles, expectations and tolerance levels of those who live there.

The fact that neighbour disputes do not constitute a recognised legal category also has important implications regarding the extent to which records are kept, the kind of information that is likely to be recorded and also its format, accessibility and retrievability for research purposes.

Data collection problems

There is no single agency with overall responsibility for dealing with neighbour disputes. Depending on the nature and seriousness of the complaint(s), the personal circumstances of the parties involved and the tenure of the properties they live in, a neighbour dispute might involve one or more of the following agencies: the police, local authority housing, environmental health, administration and legal or social services departments, citizen's advice bureaus, racial equality councils, community mediation service (if available), solicitors and either the civil or criminal courts.

The number and range of agencies that might be called upon to deal with neighbour disputes has obvious resource implications, but is also a source of difficulty for those seeking to undertake research in this area. For the purposes of this project we were asked to concentrate on just three sets of agencies: community mediation services, and local authority housing and environmental health departments; but

LIVERPOOL J... UNI... UNIVERSITY
LEARNING SERVICES

it needs to be remembered that, in seeking to quantify the scale of the problem and identify the costs of current procedures, we are only providing part of a very much larger picture.

Nor is there any centralised system for recording statistics on neighbour disputes per se and the way they are dealt with, in the way that crime statistics are compiled by the Home Office.[2] The only partial exception relates to noise nuisance complaints, which are readily accessible since the Chartered Institute of Environmental Health (CIEH) collects figures for these from local authority environmental health departments annually. This data is subsequently published both in the CIEH's own annual report and in the Digest of Environmental Statistics (Department of the Environment, 1996). However, these relate to only one category of neighbour disputes and, as we shall see, there is a serious problem of under-recording. Moreover, they are less informative about any action that might be taken by environmental health departments and its outcomes.

Although the police are frequently called to deal with neighbour disputes, they have considerable discretion in deciding how to respond to an incident, including whether or not to record it. There is little research on the way neighbour disputes are handled by the police, but Kemp et al. (1992) have suggested (p. 19) that their overriding aim is a peace-keeping one with an emphasis on effecting a temporary solution with minimum delay and repercussions for themselves.[3]

In the majority of incidents investigated[4] by Kemp et al., either no action was taken or there was only a threat of police action. Moreover, in those cases where formal police action is resorted to, the incident would be categorised under the appropriate Home Office code for the specific offence involved. Consequently, the official criminal statistics are of very limited assistance in ascertaining either the number of neighbour disputes with which the police are called upon to deal or their resource implications for the police.[5]

As for the remaining agencies, with the exception of community mediation services, neighbour disputes do not form part of their core activities. This has obvious implications for the kind of information that is recorded in relation to neighbour disputes and the way they are dealt with, and also its accessibility, comparability and utility for research purposes.

For example, local authority housing departments are primarily concerned with enforcing tenancy conditions, including those prohibiting various forms of nuisance affecting their neighbours. As we shall see, individual housing departments vary considerably in the amount of information they record, the way this is categorised and also the format in which it is held (computerised or paper records). In some departments, such information is recorded centrally while in others it is only entered onto the property files in local housing department area offices.

Even where local authority housing departments do keep central records, few of them routinely monitor either the resource costs to the department that result from neighbour disputes or the effectiveness of their procedures for responding to neighbour nuisance complaints. Consequently, one of the main problems confronting those attempting to investigate the problem of neighbour disputes and the way these are dealt with by local authority housing departments is a dearth of reliable and comparable data.

Moreover, recent changes in the legal and financial climate in which local authority housing service departments are required to operate have rendered the problem even more acute; particularly when the research focus is directed towards the issue of 'cost effectiveness'. With the advent of 'compulsory competitive tendering' requirements, the financial data that is required in order to identify the actual resource costs involved has come increasingly to be seen as 'commercially sensitive information', and this has significantly affected the willingness of individual housing departments (and their colleagues in Finance) to grant access even to the data that is available.

Some departments were reluctant even to participate in our general questionnaire survey for this reason,[6] and few were willing to put themselves forward as 'case studies' for more detailed investigations. Those that did agree insisted (for entirely understandable reasons) on absolute confidentiality, and the time taken to negotiate access and the terms on which this might be granted seriously disrupted our original schedule for completing the project.

LIVERPOOL JOHN MOORES UNIVERSITY
LEARNING SERVICES

These problems over the reliability, accessibility and comparability of data relating to neighbour disputes are serious enough in their own right, but they also contribute to the methodological problems associated with a project of this kind.

Methodological problems

The difficulties associated with cost benefit analysis in any sphere of activity are well known. The methodology it involves is complicated, and attempts to quantify any non-monetary costs and benefits that might be involved can be highly problematic. The problems are particularly acute when the technique is applied to activities in the public sector[7] (HM Treasury, 1984) since most public sector output is not sold and the benefits secured may also be difficult to measure.

Assessing the *costs* of public sector agency activities can be equally problematic, particularly where the outputs are highly individualised and variable. In the case of local authority housing departments, for example, the response to a neighbour dispute might range from sending a warning letter to rehousing the complainant or seeking to evict the person whose behaviour is complained of.

The problems are compounded when attempting to use the technique not simply to evaluate a specific project or initiative but to compare the potential costs and benefits that might be associated with a range of different approaches. They become even more acute when these approaches are as disparate as community-based mediation on the one hand, and the variety of legal, administrative and managerial techniques that are deployed by local authority housing and environmental health service departments on the other hand.

As we shall see, the process of mediation differs from most conventional responses to neighbour disputes in terms of its aims and objectives, methods and approaches and also outcomes. Moreover, its location in the voluntary sector, with all that that entails by way of resource costs and funding arrangements poses additional problems. One of the biggest methodological difficulties to be confronted is thus how to compare two sets of processes that on the surface at least appear, in many respects, to be simply incommensurable.

The combined effect of the data collection problems we have examined, together with these methodological difficulties need to be taken into account in developing a framework within which to undertake any kind of comparative cost benefit analysis in the field of neighbour disputes. As Osborn has pointed out in the slightly different but related context of public sector crime prevention, 'it is important to recognise from the outset that these assessments are bound to be rather imprecise' (Safe Neighbourhoods Unit, 1993: 143).

Rather than aiming at a precise balance-sheet approach, therefore, a more realistic objective might be to try to convey a sense of the costs and benefits involved and their relative scale. In developing our own approach we have sought to combine some of the quantitative techniques associated with conventional cost benefit analysis with a more qualitative approach that is sensitive to their limitations.

Project aims and approach, and structure of the report

One preliminary aim of the project was to review the data that is currently available relating to the number and types of neighbour disputes, and to supplement this by means of a questionnaire survey directed at local authority housing and environmental service departments. We report on this aspect of the project in Chapter 2. In Chapters 3 and 4 we look at the way neighbour disputes are dealt with, focusing specifically on the role of housing and environmental services and also that of the community mediation services, most of which operate in the voluntary sector.

One of the main aims of the project was to identify the costs incurred as a result of neighbour disputes, and to quantify these as far as possible within the limitations imposed by the quality of the data that is available. These issues are addressed in Chapters 5 to 8.

In Chapter 5 we set out to assess the human and economic costs of neighbour disputes on the parties themselves. No two neighbour disputes are exactly alike, and the effects on the individuals concerned will be highly variable. Many of the costs are not quantifiable at all, and those that are will often be unique to those involved. Consequently, it is almost impossible to generalise about the costs that are involved in neighbour disputes.

Instead, we begin by identifying the main kinds of costs that neighbour disputes might inflict on those most directly concerned. After briefly reviewing the very limited data that is available (which relates solely to the impact of neighbour noise on those who are affected by it), we attempt to illustrate the kind and range of costs that may be incurred in the course of various forms of neighbour disputes. In doing so, we draw extensively on a series of case histories, some of which are derived from media reports and some from our own analysis.

In Chapters 6 and 7 we switch the focus to local authority housing departments and the costs that can be incurred, first when neighbour disputes are dealt with by means of informal responses, and secondly on the relatively infrequent occasions where formal legal remedies are invoked. Once again we begin by identifying the kinds of costs that have to be borne by local authority housing departments.

As in Chapter 5, our approach here is based on the use of case histories since there is no such thing as an 'average' response to a neighbour dispute. However, we have also attempted to overcome some of the data collection problems that have hitherto ruled out any cost benefit analysis in relation to neighbour disputes by undertaking a more detailed case study of the actual direct costs incurred by a single area housing office when dealing with neighbour disputes over a twelve month period.

When it comes to those cases that are dealt with by means of formal legal remedies (dealt with in Chapter 7), the legal costs that are incurred are very much easier to quantify, since the 'client' departments are charged for time spent, and moreover the range of costs involved is somewhat more generalisable.

In Chapter 8 we report on a case study involving a large environmental services department in which we again attempt to determine the actual direct costs incurred in dealing with neighbour disputes over a twelve month period.

In Chapter 9 we attempt to assess the costs involved when neighbour disputes are dealt with by mediation and, within the limitations of the available data, seek to compare the effectiveness of mediation compared with the conventional approaches that are deployed by local authority housing departments and environmental services. This involves a combination of qualitative assessments and cost benefit

analysis. The latter is based on the case study data referred to above, concerning the inputs, outputs and relative costs that are associated with the various ways of responding to neighbour disputes.

In Chapter 10 we consider some of the policy implications suggested by the project's findings, and make suggestions for further research.

Notes

1   But not exclusively. The courts have also defined the term 'neighbour' very restrictively in the past. For example a County Court judge in Woolwich ruled that Asians with shops situated 350 yards from the defendant's flat, and who had been subjected to racial harassment including violent attack and a campaign of intimidation were not 'neighbours' of the defendant for the purpose of possession proceedings (Madge, 1996: 12) although, as we shall see in Chapter 3 (pp. 23ff), the law itself has now been changed.

2   The limitations of official crime statistics as a measure of how many crimes are committed are well known, but the absence of any comprehensive system for recording even those neighbour disputes that are reported to the police or local authority housing departments makes it virtually impossible to quantify the scale of the problem.

3   It should be noted that, in contrast to the situation in England and Wales, the police in Scotland do have powers to tackle certain noise problems (Department of the Environment, 1995).

4   These included domestic disputes and other small-scale interpersonal disputes as well as neighbour disputes.

5   Indeed, the impact of neighbour disputes on police resource costs, and the potential for savings to be made by involving community mediation services in appropriate cases would merit further investigation in their own right.

6   The commonest reason given for being unable to respond to the survey was lack of time/other priorities (cited by 6 Housing Departments).

7   A very useful review of the use and limitations of cost benefit analysis in the sphere of crime prevention and related public sector activities is provided by Osborn (Safe Neighbourhoods Unit, 1993).

How many neighbour disputes?

Quantifying the scale of the problem is difficult, and some of the organisational reasons for this have been identified in the previous chapter. In the following section we will be drawing on data obtained from the following sources:

- 'Good neighbours survey' – report of a national study commissioned by General Accident in 1995, based on a representative sample of 1062 people aged 16 or over who were interviewed during September and October 1995 (cited as General Accident, 1995);

- National Noise Attitude Survey conducted in 1991 by the Building Research Establishment, based on face-to-face interviews with a random sample of 2,373 people aged 16 or over selected from the electoral register for 157 sampling areas throughout Great Britain (cited as BRE study). The findings of the survey are reported in the Digest of Environmental Statistics (Department of the Environment, 1996);

- Annual Survey of noise complaints received by local authority Environmental Health Officers compiled by the Chartered Institute of Environmental Health and reported in the Digest of Environmental Statistics (Department of the Environment, 1996);

- Data obtained from our own general survey of a sample of Housing Departments and Environmental Health Service Departments conducted as part of the present research.

How many neighbour disputes? Existing data and project findings

A recent national survey (General Accident, 1995) exploring people's attitudes towards their neighbours reported that 1 in 5 (20%) admitted to having been involved in 'a heated exchange of words' with their neighbours. Over 1 in 14 (7%) claimed to have reported a neighbour to the police, and 6% to the environmental health department. Only 1 in 25 (4%) complained of having bad neighbours and deliberately seeking to avoid them. A similar proportion (4%) had threatened to take legal action against a neighbour, though only 1% claimed to have carried out the threat and taken a neighbour to court. Although the findings suggest that conflict between neighbours is confined to a relatively small minority of householders, when extrapolated to the population at large the numbers involved are likely to be very substantial indeed. On average, these figures suggest that for every residential street there might be at least one set of neighbours whose relationship is problematic, though in practice the survey found that relations between neighbours were likely to be poorer for people living in flats/maisonettes and in privately rented accommodation. The main sources of conflict disclosed by the survey[1] are shown in Table 2.1.

The biggest source of conflict between neighbours was undoubtedly noise of various kinds. The most frequently mentioned neighbour nuisance was barking dogs, which 21% of those questioned claimed to experience on occasion. This was closely followed by loud stereo or radio music and parking in front of the house (mentioned by 20% and 19% of respondents respectively). Noisy DIY work and noisy children were each mentioned by 13% of respondents while 8% said they had experienced overhanging trees, and 6% complained of rubbish, rubble or car parts being left in front of a neighbour's house.

The extent to which people are affected by noise of different kinds, and their attitudes towards it, has also been monitored. As part of a national noise awareness and attitude survey conducted in 1991 (BRE study), people were asked to indicate whether they heard noise from any of 49 itemised sources while they were at home, and how they were affected by them. The results are published in the Digest of Environmental Statistics (Department of the Environment, para. 6.3 and Table 6.1) and are shown in Table 2.2 below.

Noise made by neighbours was the third most commonly heard category of noise,[2] and was mentioned by 24% of respondents.[3] However it generated a higher proportion of objections relative to those who could hear it than the two most frequently encountered sources of noise (road traffic and aircraft noise). Moreover, of all the noise sources mentioned, neighbour noise was most likely to cause annoyance on occasion (mentioned by 72% of those who heard it), and was most likely to be considered a nuisance (mentioned by 73% of those who heard it).

Another source of information about the scale of the problem constituted by neighbour noise is provided by the annual returns relating to the number of complaints received by local authority Environmental Health Officers (EHOs) which are compiled by the Chartered Institute of Environmental Health (CIEH) (Department of the Environment 1996, para. 6.11 and Tables 6.7 and 6.10). Table 2.3 below shows how the proportion of domestic noise complaints received by Environmental Health Officers compares with all other categories of noise complaints in recent years.

Noise from domestic premises constitutes by far the commonest category of complaints to local

authority EHOs, and in 1993/4 accounted for 69% of all complaints received (compared with 54% in 1982). The actual number of complaints has increased more than four-fold since 1980, and now stands at 131,153, representing 3,468 complaints per million inhabitants.[4]

Not all noise complaints are indicative of neighbour disputes since some complaints may relate to 'one-off' incidents such as burglar alarms, or complaints about barking dogs where it is not known who the owner is. To some extent, therefore, the figures compiled by the Chartered Institute of

Table 2.1: Main sources of conflict between neighbours.

Form of nuisance	Capacity in which experienced	
	as 'victim' %	as 'perpetrator' %
Barking dogs	21	8
Loud stereo or radio music	20	13
Parking in front of the house	19	4
Noisy DIY work	13	5
Noisy children	13	9
Overhanging trees	8	3
Rubbish/rubble/car parts etc. in front of the house	6	1
Banging on the wall when they/you are noisy	6	3
None of these	45	66
Don't know	2	3

Source of data: General Accident 'Good Neighbours Survey'

Table 2.2: National Noise Attitude Survey 1991: source of noise and effects on those who heard it.

Source of noise	Number who[1] heard noise	Percentage[2] affected who:					
		Objected to noise	Were irritated by noise	Were disturbed by it at times	Were concerned at times by it	Were annoyed by it at times	Considered noise a nuisance
Road traffic	1,117	67	79	83	58	63	63
Aircraft	969	48	67	76	41	47	49
Neighbours	572	72	89	86	51	72	73
Trains	306	43	71	78	31	50	49
Other people nearby	302	74	86	88	53	69	68
Sports events	125	26	67	59	30	41	41
Building construction or roadworks	110	52	79	75	33	57	48
Entertainments or leisure	97	75	94	86	62	69	73
Farming or agriculture	81	42	74	90	26	53	32
Factories or works	52	57	70	65	43	60	38
Commercial premises	47	74	80	77	52	56	68

[1] Actual number of respondents who heard noise from this source from a total number of 2,373
[2] Percentage based on number of respondents who heard noise from this source
Source of data: Building Research Establishment National Noise Attitude Survey (Department of the Environment 1996, Table 6.1)

Table 2.3: Domestic noise and other categories of noise complaints received by Environmental Health Officers at selected intervals between 1982-1993/4.

England and Wales	Number per million people			
	1982	1986/7	1990/1	1993/4
Controlled by relevant Act				
Domestic premises	794	1269	2264	3468
Industrial or commercial premises	473	654	913	1120
Road works, construction & demolition	84	153	252	168
Controlled by s. 62 of the Act				
Noise in streets	46	55	75	92
Not controlled by relevant Acts				
All sources (road traffic, aircraft, other)	69	114	140	207
Total complaints received	1466	2245	3644	5055

Source of data: Adapted from Digest of Environmental Statistics 1996, Table 6.7
(Department of the Environment, 1996)

Environmental Health may slightly over-inflate the total volume of recorded noise-related neighbour disputes. However, there is reason to suppose that in other respects even these figures represent only the tip of a very large iceberg since the 1991 BRE noise attitude study revealed that of those who objected to domestic noise from all sources, only 3.6% complained to the EHO.[5]

Moreover, noise complaints are not the only potential source of neighbour disputes for which EHOs are responsible. Unfortunately, there are no comparable statistics for non-noise related complaints. However, as part of our general Environ-

mental Health Services survey, we asked respondents to indicate the number of 'domestic noise' and 'other neighbour nuisance' cases received during 1994. From this it appears that on average noise nuisance complaints account for approximately two-thirds of the total, though the proportions vary according to type of council, as can be seen from Figure 2.1.[6]

If the same pattern is repeated in other councils across the country, there could be up to 44,000 non-noise related domestic nuisance complaints in addition to the 131,153 noise-related complaints which are recorded by EHOs each year.

The survey also sought information about the types of neighbour nuisance cases referred to EHOs, and this is set out in Figure 2.2.[7] Respondents were asked to indicate either the number or proportion of complaints relating to different types of behaviour that might be thought likely to cause offence.[8] Once again, noise-related complaints account for almost two-thirds of the total volume, followed by other forms of dog nuisance (16%), complaints relating to gardens (13%) or to communal areas (11%).

For those living in local authority accommodation, an alternative channel for complaints about neighbour nuisance is the council's Housing Department (or Housing Association). However, in the absence of any reliable national data, it is impossible to know how many complaints are made each year to the country's 'social landlords'. Only a minority (11) of the 24 landlords[9] participating in our companion Housing Services survey monitored the number of neighbour nuisance complaints they received. Altogether, the eleven departments received a total of 12,065 cases in 1994, which averages out at 1,193 for each department. This is only slightly fewer than the average number of domestic noise complaints per Environmental Health department (1,281). If the pattern is similar for other councils across the country, our findings suggest that local authority housing departments and housing associations could be receiving

Figure 2.1: Relative proportion of domestic noise complaints and other forms of neighbour nuisance received by EHOs in 1994 by type of council.

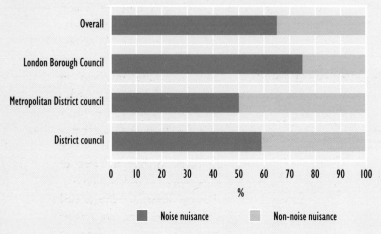

Source of data: Mediation research project national survey of Environmental Health departments

upwards of 100,000 neighbour nuisance complaints per year. However, these calculations should be treated with caution in view of the relatively small size of the sample and the large variations in the average number of complaints received each year according to the type of council, as can be seen from Table 2.4.[10]

Only eight of the eleven Housing Departments[11] taking part in the survey were able to provide us with information indicating the types of behaviour complained of (see Figure 2.3). Although noise complaints still predominated, (accounting for 42.5% of all complaints), property abuse and personal conflict were also significant causes for complaint (accounting for 16.3% and 16.1% of all complaints respectively).

Conclusions: putting the problem of neighbour disputes into perspective

It would be impossible to quantify the actual volume of neighbour disputes in England and Wales. The only national statistics that are available relate to noise complaints and, as we have attempted to show, such is the scale of under-reporting that these are unlikely to provide an accurate measure of even those neighbour disputes that involve complaints about noise. To these must be added those non-noise related neighbour disputes that are also reported to Environmental Health Departments but which are not collated and published; plus those neighbour nuisance complaints involving the tenants of social landlords which, likewise, are not centrally collated and published.

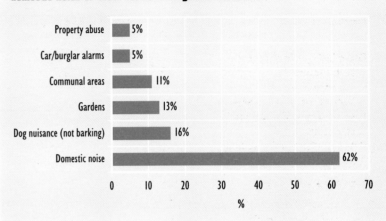

Figure 2.2: Classification of complaints to local authority EHOs involving domestic noise or other forms of neighbour nuisance.

Source of data: Mediation research project national survey of Environmental Health departments

Based on our survey findings, our 'best estimate'[12] of the total number of neighbour nuisance complaints within each of these categories in England and Wales is as follows:

- domestic noise complaints recorded by Environmental Health depts: 131,153

- other non-noise related complaints recorded by Env't Health depts: 40,000

- neighbour nuisance complaints recorded by Housing depts: 100,000

- Estimated total number of neighbour nuisance complaints recorded by the above agencies   271,153

Some neighbour nuisance complaints may involve both housing and environmental health services, so to that extent the above figures may over-inflate the number of separate complaints each year. However, some of those involved in neighbour disputes may refer the matter to the police, either as well as, or as an alternative to reporting it to one of the above agencies. Although some of these will be recorded as crimes, the way these are categorised unfortunately does not enable the number of neighbour

Table 2.4: Number of allegations of neighbour nuisance received by different types of local council housing departments.

Type of council	Number of departments	Smallest number	Largest number	Average number
City Council	2	700	3600	2150
District/Borough Council	4	183	1750	637
Metropolitan District Council	3	116	680	527
London Borough Council	1	–	–	3500
Housing Association	1	–	–	137

Source of data: Mediation research project national survey of local authority housing departments

disputes the police are involved in to be easily calculated. A few of those embroiled in neighbour disputes will attempt to resolve the matter by initiating legal proceedings but probably the great majority will either seek to deal with the dispute informally themselves, or will simply attempt to endure the conflict.

Next we will examine in more detail the way neighbour disputes are dealt with, by complainants; and also by local authority housing and environmental health services when complaints about neighbour nuisance are made to them.

Notes

1   Respondents were asked 'Which of the following do your neighbours ever inflict on you?' They were also asked to indicate which of the nuisances they were ever guilty of inflicting on their neighbours.

2   After road traffic and aircraft, which were mentioned by 47% and 41% of respondents respectively.

3   If noise from other people nearby is also included, the proportion who were affected increases to 37%.

4   The most up to date figures show a further increase in the number of noise complaints recorded by EHOs in 1994/5 to 144,943 which represents 3,949 complaints per million inhabitants. [Source: direct communication from the Department of the Environment].

5   Figure calculated from Dept of the Environment, 1996: Table 6.6.

6   We have compiled this based on the average numbers of complaints in each category, though five of the 22 councils involved in the survey were unable to provide us with information relating to non-noise cases, and one council did not keep central records relating to either category of complaint.

7   Unfortunately, councils are not consistent in the way they record and categorise data relating to non-noise complaints. The number of returns on which the mean proportions have been calculated varies for each category of behaviour, and consequently the proportions do not add up to 100 per cent.

8   We cannot be sure that all of these involved a dispute between neighbours since, for example, reports relating to car or burglar alarms could well relate to one-off incidents, and might even reflect neighbourly concern. Likewise, in the case of complaints about stray or barking dogs, it might not be apparent who owns the animal.

9   Comprising 22 Housing Departments and 2 Housing Associations.

10 It should also be noted that none of the councils taking part in the survey were 'shire' counties, where the number of neighbour nuisance cases might be expected to be smaller than in the case of the predominantly urban district, metropolitan and London councils that responded to the survey.

11 Comprising 2 City Councils, 2 District Councils, 1 Metropolitan District Council, 1 London Borough Council and 2 Housing Associations.

12 The following figures should be read in the light of the accompanying 'health warnings' referred to already.

Figure 2.3: Types of neighbour nuisance complaints received by social landlords.

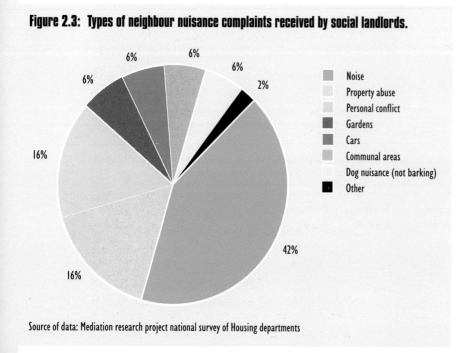

Source of data: Mediation research project national survey of Housing departments

Tackling neighbour disputes: how are they dealt with?

Action taken by complainants to resolve neighbour disputes or noise complaints

People who are involved in conflicts with their neighbours are much more likely to either take no action or seek to resolve the matter informally rather than to make a complaint to the police or other agency. In a recent national survey (General Accident, 1995), the great majority (89%) said that they would attempt to deal with the matter by way of a friendly word or letter (see Table 3.1). Only 2% of the total would threaten to report their neighbour to the local authority or the police while only 1% indicated that they would think of threatening legal action in the first instance. However, over one in three of those questioned felt that it should be easier to prosecute bad neighbours (36% agreed strongly), and over half believed that local authorities and/or the police should have stronger powers to prosecute bad neighbours (54% agreed strongly).

A similar preference for informal action was recorded by the 1991 national noise awareness and attitude survey (BRE survey; see Dept. of the Environment, 1996), which asked people what action they took in response to neighbour noise disturbance; though in the majority of cases no action of any kind was taken (Table 3.2).

On average, around one in five people indicated that they had complained directly to the

person responsible for the noise. Of the formal agencies, people were almost as likely to complain about noise to the police as to their local council, and of those who did contact the council, many were unable to specify which department was involved. Where the department was identified, however, it appears that complaints about noise are as likely to be reported to the Housing Department as to the Environmental Health Officer. Once again, very few sought legal advice or took legal action.

How neighbour nuisance complaints are dealt with: Local Authority Environmental Health Services

Under current legislation,[1] local authorities have wide-ranging powers to deal with a variety of neighbour nuisance complaints, including noise from premises and in the street, accumulations and deposits, smoke and animals (see Karn et al., 1993: 92 for details). Powers relating to the control of neighbour noise have been extended further by the Noise Act 1996,[2] which will introduce a new offence of night-time noise from domestic premises and clarifies local authority powers with respect to the seizure and disposal of noise-making equipment. Nevertheless, in many, or indeed most neighbour disputes, the existing controls may be all but irrelevant (Karn et al., 1993: 96).

One major drawback is the judgmental nature of the statutory nuisance controls, which can often lead to prolonged arguments once a case reaches the court. This, coupled with an increasing general reluctance on the part of many complainants to appear in court as witnesses, leads to an expensive and cumbersome procedure which is only likely to be invoked where the behaviour complained of is gross, and all other attempts at alternative resolution have failed. Moreover, it is often not the end of the matter since the primary objective is not to resolve the

Table 3.1: How people believe conflicts with neighbours can best be resolved.

Preferred course of action to resolve conflict with neighbours	Total %
Friendly word or letter	89
Strong words/ strongly worded letter	4
Threats to report neighbour to the local authority/police	2
Threats of legal action	1
None of these	2
Don't know	2

Source of data: General Accident 'Good Neighbours Survey'

Table 3.2: Action taken by complainants in response to neighbour noise disturbance: 1991.

Noise source	No.who objected to noise	Percentage of those who objected who took type of action:									
		Take no action	Complain to person making noise	Complain to police	Complain to L.A. (unspec-ified)	Complain to EHO	Complain to Housing Dept.	Take legal advice or action	Petition	Complain to MP or Councillor	Install double glazing
People's voices	161	59	23	14	8	3	4	2	3	0	4
Radio/TV/Hi-Fi	149	58	29	5	6	3	4	1	0	0	4
Animal noise	145	69	24	2	3	6	3	0	1	0	1
Children	122	57	31	10	6	1	1	0	0	1	5
Neighbours' vehicles	88	63	18	9	10	6	3	0	0	0	8
Door-banging	83	65	24	2	8	6	6	0	0	0	4
D.I.Y.	64	77	17	2	2	3	2	0	0	0	2
Lawn mowers	31	97	3	0	0	0	0	0	0	0	0
Footsteps	26	69	8	8	4	0	4	0	4	0	8
Domestic appliances	20	70	20	5	0	0	0	0	0	0	0

Source of data: Building Research Establishment National Noise Attitude Survey reported in Digest of Environment Statistics Table 6.6

dispute between the parties, but to enforce compliance with the legislation and, as we shall see, even that is not always successful.

As can be seen from Table 3.3, in 1993/4 there were almost four complaints for every nuisance confirmed, and only around one in three sources were considered to constitute a nuisance. An abatement notice was issued in only 4.8% of sources (around one in twenty). Fewer than 10% of these resulted in prosecutions, and in only 7.5% of cases where an abatement notice was served was a conviction obtained. The fact that so few complaints result in a conviction (0.28%, which represents just under 1% of confirmed nuisance cases) probably heightens complainants' perceptions that little can be done about the problem, and is an important consideration to bear in mind when comparing the effectiveness of this approach with that of mediation.

It is not clear from the nationally available statistics referred to above what informal actions are taken by Environmental Health Officers in response to neighbour nuisance complaints, and this is something we set out to investigate by means of our general survey of selected Environmental Health Service Departments, supplemented by a more detailed case study of one Environmental Health Service department that was not included in the general survey.[4]

Respondents were asked to indicate what proportion of neighbour nuisance complaints[5] received by the department were investigated by an Environmental Health Officer. The great majority of departments (87%) claimed to investigate more than 95% of all complaints received, and 13 of them claimed to investigate all complaints.[6] It should be noted that section 79 of the Environmental Protection Act 1990 places a duty on local authorities to take all steps that are reasonably practicable to investigate a complaint of statutory nuisance from someone living in their area. However, one respondent indicated that in many cases the 'investigation' might amount to no more than a letter to both parties. We suspect that the same is probably true of many other respondents, particularly in view of the much smaller proportion of cases in which visits were made to one or other of the parties.

The type of action taken by Environmental Health Service departments in response to neighbour nuisance complaints is shown in Table 3.4. The very small proportion of cases resulting in any kind of formal action is very much in line with the national statistics which we refer to above. Of the informal responses, the commonest by far was the sending of an advisory letter to complainants. However the overall average of 68.6% for this response masked some variations both according to type of council (see Table 3.4), and also between individual councils of the same type.

For example, in many councils 90% or more of complainants were sent an advisory letter; but while this applied to five out of the seven District Councils and four out of the five Metropolitan

District Councils, only one of the six London Borough Councils recorded a percentage as high as this. Conversely, other councils were much more restrained in their use of advisory letters, particularly in the case of the London Borough Councils, some of which recorded percentages as low as 3%, 16% and 18%.

Just over half of all complainants (56%) received a visit from the local Environmental Health Officer. Here again there were considerable variations between types of department and even within departments of the same type. In general complainants were more likely to receive an advisory letter than to be visited by an EHO, except in London where two-thirds of complainants resulted in a visit and only slightly under one-half were sent an advisory letter.

Visits were made to the alleged perpetrator of the nuisance in just under half of all complaints. Here there was less variation between the different types of council, though there was still considerable disparity within councils of the same type (ranging from 3% to 95% in the case of District councils for example). Warning letters were sent to the alleged perpetrators of the nuisance in 41% of all complaints.

As for the remaining informal responses, a small minority of cases (6%) was referred on to some other agency apart from mediation. We will comment on the use and potential use of mediation in more detail in a later section, but it is striking how few cases were referred for mediation, even allowing for the fact that half the departments in the sample did not have access to a mediation service. If these are excluded from the analysis, the proportion of complaints referred for mediation was still only 2.5%, and in none of the eight councils with access to such a service was it greater than 5%. This could be partly explained by the fact that local authorities are aware of their duty under section 80 of the 1990 Act to serve an abatement notice where they are

Table 3.3[3]: Action taken by Environmental Health Officers in response to domestic noise complaints: 1982–1993/4.

England and Wales Year	Numbers, rates and percentages						
	1982	1984/5	1986/7	1988/9	1990/1	1992/3	1993/4
No. of complaints	33,014	48,645	46,803	59,061	88,263	111,515	131,153
Complaints per million pop.	794	1,244	1,269	1,620	2,264	3,137	3,468
Sources complained of	23,951	33,736	29,223	35,748	50,456	83,164	106,721
No. of nuisances confirmed	11,690	15,231	13,626	16,788	20,041	40,096	37,209
Abatement notices served	1,073	2,156	1,763	1,865	3,119	3,673	5,054
Prosecutions	-	-	-	-	-	-	441
Convictions	-	-	-	-	-	-	372
Percentage of sources considered a nuisance	48.8	45.1	46.6	47.0	39.7	45.6	34.5
percentage of sources for which an abatement notice was served	4.5	6.4	6.0	5.2	6.2	4.3	4.8

Source of data: CIEH reported in Digest of Environment Statistics Table 6.10

satisfied that there is evidence of a statutory nuisance, but as we have seen (in Table 3.4), only around one in twenty cases is dealt with in this way.

In general, the data derived from our general survey of Environmental Health Service departments serves to confirm the impression conveyed by the national statistics that in dealing with neighbour nuisance cases very little use is made of the available statutory powers. Indeed, in very many cases it appears that the only response is an advisory letter to the complainant setting out the very limited circumstances in which the department might be prepared to take action. Even then, this is unlikely to involve more than a visit to one or both parties and, possibly, a warning letter to the alleged perpetrator of the nuisance.

How neighbour nuisance complaints are dealt with: Local Authority Housing Services

Acting in their capacity as social landlords, local authority Housing Services departments (and Housing Associations) have a number of additional legal and administrative powers to deal with the problem of neighbour nuisance involving their tenants (see generally, Karn et al., 1993). They include the strategy of seeking to secure compliance with tenancy agreements, which frequently include 'no nuisance' clauses, either by means of persuasion

Table 3.4: Proportion of cases[7] resulting in different types of action by Environmental Health Service Departments

Type of action	District	Metropolitan	LBC	Overall
No action	2.0 (9)	0.0 (2)	6.0 (6)	3.1 (17)
Send advisory letter to complainant	75.5 (7)	83.2 (5)	48.5 (6)	68.6 (18)
Visit(s) to complainant	46.5 (7)	54.8 (4)	66.5 (6)	56.1 (17)
Visit(s) to alleged perpetrator	50.0 (7)	52.0 (4)	42.0 (6)	47.8 (17)
Send warning letter to alleged 'perpetrator'	57.9 (7)	35.2 (3)	27.9 (7)	41.5 (17)
Refer to mediation	0.8 (5)	1.6 (3)	1.8 (7)	1.4 (15)
Refer to other agency	3.6 (6)	5.0 (2)	10.4 (5)	6.4 (13)
Serve abatement notice	5.8 (8)	3.6 (4)	7.4 (6)	5.7 (18)
Prosecute for non-compliance	0.4 (7)	0.3 (5)	1.1 (6)	0.6 (18)
Conviction obtained	0.4 (7)	0.3 (5)	1.0 (6)	0.6 (18)
Apply for injunction	0.0 (7)	0.0 (3)	0.0 (6)	0.0 (16)
Prosecute for breach of bye-laws	0.0 (4)	0.0 (3)	0.0 (6)	0.0 (13)

Source of data: Mediation research project national survey of Environmental Health departments

or the threat of legal action. A recent innovation is the introduction of 'introductory' or 'probationary tenancies' under the Housing Act 1996,[8] the effect of which is to defer for a year secure tenancy status and protection. They are intended to make it easier for social landlords to gain possession of the property if a tenant causes problems during the first twelve months of a tenancy.

Ultimately, a social landlord may seek to evict a seriously disruptive tenant by seeking a possession order through the courts. Alternatively (or in conjunction with an application for possession), an injunction may be sought to secure compliance with a specific tenancy condition. Once again the existing powers enabling social landlords to obtain injunctions will be strengthened as a result of the Housing Act 1996.[9] Another possibility is to rely on the voluntary transfer of one of the parties.

As with statutory nuisance proceedings, however, there are problems with all these approaches. Legal remedies are expensive to pursue, involve difficult evidential issues (including a reluctance on the part of some complainants to appear as witnesses for fear of retaliation), and tend to be unpredictable in outcome because of the high level of proof involved.[10] Moreover, problems have arisen in the past when seeking to enforce tenancy obligations where someone other than the tenant is responsible for the nuisance. Conversely, some local authorities may be reluctant to become involved when the complainant is not a tenant of theirs. This is likely to

cause problems particularly in areas where large numbers of former tenants have exercised the right to buy their homes from the council.

Under Part V of the Housing Act 1996, changes have been introduced to simplify the procedure by which social landlords may seek possession against anti-social tenants, and also significantly to extend the grounds on which possession may be sought. In particular, possession may now be granted[11] whether the person responsible for the nuisance or annoyance resides in or is simply a visitor to a dwelling-house.

Moreover, it is no longer necessary to prove (for example by producing witnesses) that nuisance or annoyance has actually been caused to anyone since the new test merely requires that the behaviour complained of 'is likely to cause' nuisance or annoyance to a person 'residing, visiting or otherwise engaging in lawful activity in the locality'. Under this new formulation possession may be granted where nuisance or annoyance is caused to people who are not neighbours of those responsible, such as housing officers (Madge, 1996: 12). In spite of these changes, possession proceedings are still likely to prove expensive and uncertain remedies, since courts will need to be satisfied, as in the past, that it is reasonable to make the order, and in many cases tenants will seek to exploit both the many technical and substantive defences that remain available to them and their advisers (see Karn et al., 1993: 141-2).

Relying on voluntary transfers may also have significant cost implications and, as in the case of compulsory evictions, does nothing to address or resolve the disruptive behaviour itself. The problem may simply be moved to a new location, or, where the complainant is transferred, may continue to plague the new occupants. Indeed, additional problems may be caused if too many 'respectable' tenants apply for transfer in response to anti-social behaviour since this can all too easily affect the reputation and desirability of the area. Adjacent properties may become difficult or impossible to let and, in extreme cases, it is not unknown for drastic action to be taken, including demolition.

Even introductory tenancies have their critics (Cornwell, 1995). They are only applicable to tenants whose behaviour causes problems within the first twelve months of their occupancy and fears have been expressed that they may tip the balance unfairly in favour of the secure tenant in any dispute. Tenants do have a right to request a review of the landlord's decision to seek possession (which courts are obliged to grant if the notice is unchallenged), as provided for in the Introductory Tenants (Review) Regulations 1996.

Although previous research (Karn, et al., 1993: 15) has established that most landlords rely solely on tenancy agreements when seeking to deal with neighbour disputes, relatively little is known of the way local authority housing departments use their formal powers or what informal action they might take in response to neighbour nuisance complaints. In part this is because there is no equivalent monitoring procedure to that undertaken by the Chartered Institute of Environmental Health and compiled by the Department of the Environment in respect of domestic noise complaints received by Environmental Health Officers. An even bigger problem is that relatively few social landlords themselves monitor the number of neighbour nuisance complaints they receive, and even fewer keep central records of the way these cases are dealt with.

In one recent survey (Aldbourne Associates, 1993: 2), only eight out of 47 landlords surveyed recorded such information, or the amount of staff time which is spent on neighbour nuisance and related problems. In our own questionnaire survey of local authority housing departments only 11 of the 24 landlords who responded monitored the number of neighbour nuisance cases they received, and not all of these were able to provide us with detailed information relating to the way these cases were dealt with.[12]

The information that was provided is presented in Table 3.5, and is expressed as a percentage of the number of allegations received, together with the number (and type) of local authority housing departments upon which this information is based (given in brackets). It should be remembered that each case can result in more than one of these action types.

The table shows that local authority housing departments make almost as little use of their formal legal powers as do their counterparts in Environmental Health,[13] which is unsurprising in view of the problems referred to above, and also the somewhat drastic nature of the 'remedies' themselves. Likewise, the administrative procedure involving a transfer of tenancy is also used in only a tiny proportion of cases, and is much more likely to be invoked on behalf of the complainant rather than the alleged perpetrator of the nuisance. Consequently, there may be little that housing officers can do beyond reminding tenants of their tenancy obligations and warning of the consequences that might follow in the event of non-compliance.

Half of all complaints appear to be dealt with by means of a warning letter, and slightly over half involved a visit to the alleged perpetrator. Visits were made to complainants in over two-thirds of the cases. In a significant minority of cases either no action was taken (14%), presumably where there is no breach of the tenancy agreement or this cannot be proved, or

Table 3.5: Proportion of cases resulting in different types of action by local authority Housing Departments/Housing Associations

Type	District	MDC	LBC	Housing Assoc.	Overall
No action	10.0 (2)	10.0 (1)	40.0 (1)	0.0 (1)	14.0 (5)
Advise to take own action	11.7 (3)	10.0 (1)	20.0 (1)	12.0 (1)	12.8 (6)
Visit complainant	76.7 (3)	80.0 (1)	50.0 (1)	73.0 (1)	72.2 (6)
Visit alleged perpetrator	56.7 (3)	70.0 (1)	40.0 (1)	73.0 (1)	58.8 (6)
Send warning letter	47.5 (4)	70.0 (1)	40.0 (1)	55.0 (1)	50.7 (7)
Refer to mediation	30.0 (4)	6.5 (2)	1.5 (2)	0.0 (1)	15.1 (9)
Refer to other agency	5.0 (2)	0.0 (1)	5.0 (1)	39.0 (1)	10.8 (5)
Transfer complainant	1.7 (3)	5.0 (1)	5.0 (1)	3.0 (1)	3.0 (6)
Transfer alleged perpetrator	0.7 (3)	0.0 (2)	0.5 (1)	0.0 (1)	0.4 (7)
Served abatement notice	2.5 (2)	5.1 (2)	6.0 (1)	0.0 (1)	3.6 (6)
Prosecution for non-compliance	0.3 (2)	1.0 (2)	0.5 (1)	0.0 (1)	0.5 (6)
Convicted for non-compliance	0.0 (1)	0.0 (2)	0.2 (1)	0.0 (1)	0.04 (5)
Application for injunction	0.0 (1)	0.2 (2)	0.1 (2)	1.5 (1)	0.3 (6)
Application for possession order	2.3 (3)	1.2 (2)	0.4 (2)	31.0 (1)	5.1 (8)
Prosecuted for breach of bye-laws	0.0 (3)	0.0 (1)	0.1 (2)	0.0 (1)	0.03 (7)

Source of data: Mediation research project national survey of Housing departments

the complainant was advised to take his or her own action (13%). A much higher proportion of cases were referred for mediation overall (15%) than was found with the Environmental Health Service survey (see Table 3.4 above), though there was considerable variation between the different types of councils. In general, it appears that District Councils were very much more willing to make such referrals than other types of council.

Dealing with neighbour disputes: emerging issues

On the evidence we have been examining in this section, it appears that most neighbour disputes are dealt with informally by the parties themselves or (we suspect in many cases) not at all. Although only a relatively small proportion of disputes are referred to local authority housing or environmental health officials, the numbers involved appear to be substantial and, at least in the case of noise complaints, are increasing steadily every year.

The fact that so many complaints are dealt with by means of visits and/or warning letters suggests that dealing with neighbour disputes is likely to be a time-consuming and costly exercise for both sets of departments.[14] Just how costly is not known, since so few departments appear to monitor the process, and those that do are unlikely to make this information publicly available, especially in the changed financial climate brought about by compulsory competitive tendering.[15] We will attempt to shed some light on the *resource implications* associated with the problem of neighbour disputes in Chapters 6-8.

Another important issue that is raised by the evidence we have been examining relates to the *effectiveness* of existing strategies for dealing with neighbour disputes. Little use is made of the legal and administrative remedies that are formally available and, as we have indicated, their effectiveness is in any event also open to question. Beyond that, very little is known about the informal action that might be taken by local council officers when dealing with neighbour nuisance complaints or how this compares with the alternative approach that is offered by growing numbers of community mediation services. We will comment on the latter in Chapter 4 before we return to these issues again in Chapter 9.

In the next chapter we examine the involvement and role of community mediation services in relation to neighbour disputes.

Notes

1 Part III of the Environmental Protection Act 1990, as amended by the Noise and Statutory Nuisance Act 1993.

2 The Noise Act received Royal Assent on 18 July 1996. The clarified powers authorising confiscation of noise-making equipment came into force on 19 September 1996. Because of the need to consult fully on the technical aspects of the new night noise offence, this will not be available for local authorities to apply to their area until April 1997.

3 Adapted from Department of the Environment, 1996: Table 6.10, supplemented by additional figures relating to the number of prosecutions and convictions obtained in 1993-4, which were provided by the Chartered Institute of Environmental Health.

4 It was originally selected in order to 'pilot' the general survey questionnaire, and then agreed to co-operate with a more detailed examination of all case files opened between 1 April 1994 and 31 March 1995.

5 The questionnaire asked for either the exact number investigated, or the estimated proportion. Twenty three departments responded to this question, 12 of which provided exact figures. These were then converted into percentages.

6 The three exceptions claimed to investigate 80%, 75% and 63% respectively.

7 Number of responses on which based shown in brackets.

8 Section 124. The provision, which allows local housing authorities or Housing Action Trusts to operate an introductory tenancy regime, is due to come into effect in January 1997, and Manchester City Council will be one of the first to authorities to introduce such a regime.

9 Specifically, the new powers will enable injunctions to be granted inter alia to prevent anyone from using or threatening to use premises for immoral purposes and also to prohibit them from entering residential purposes. The new provisions are due to come into effect later in 1997 on a date which has still to be finalised.

10 Other attempts to strengthen existing legal powers for dealing with 'nuisance neighbours', such as those currently under consideration as part of a package of 'anti-stalking' measures are likely to suffer from similar limitations.

11 Set out in sections 144 and 148 of the 1996 Act.

12 More detailed information relating to the way neighbour nuisance complaints were handled by one particular housing department can be found in the detailed case study referred to on page 44ff.

13 See Table 3.4, above.

14 Some research suggests that up to 20% of housing officer's time is spent dealing with nuisance behaviour. See further discussion on page 43ff.

15 At least in relation to housing departments, since environmental health service departments are not yet affected by the new CCT regulations.

Mediation and neighbour disputes: assessing the role of community mediation services

ediation is a method of dealing with conflict by enabling people to negotiate a mutually acceptable outcome with the help of a neutral third party.[1] Although it has a long and respectable pedigree, the use of mediation as a means of resolving neighbour disputes and other forms of conflict in the community is relatively recent. As recently as 1985 there were reported to be only six Community Mediation Schemes in England and Wales, of which only 3 were operational (Marshall and Walpole, 1985; see also Davis et al., 1987).

Since then, there has been a dramatic expansion in the number of mediation services throughout the United Kingdom, particularly in the field of community mediation. At the time of our general survey in spring 1995 there were 36 established services and a further 11 which were about to become operational. However, by June 1996 the number of community mediation services that were in operation or about to start had risen to 65 (Mediation UK, 1996: 1).

In the past, lack of access to a nearby commu-nity mediation service has been a major constraint on the viability of mediation as an alternative to more traditional methods of dealing with neighbour disputes. This position appears to be changing rapidly, though there is still a considerable way to go in order to achieve the optimum density of one service for each population centre of 50,000 – 100,000 (Mediation UK, 1993: 14).

Age and status of community mediation services

Not surprisingly, the great majority of community mediation services had been in existence for less than five years, and, as can be seen from Figure 4.1, most had only become operational within the previous three years. Three of the mediation services described their status as being part of a statutory organisation while the remainder all described themselves as independent. All but two of the services were affiliated to Mediation UK, while five services were affiliated to some other organisation instead of, or in addition to, Mediation UK.

Just under half the services (14) indicated that the local authority housing department or housing association were represented on their management or steering committee, while environmental health and social service departments were each represented on the committees of five community mediation services. The organisation that is most likely to be represented on the steering or management group is the police (mentioned by 20 services).[2]

Figure 4.1: Age of Community Mediation Services.

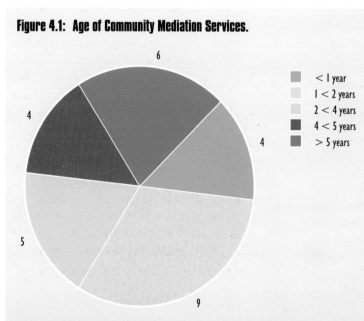

Legend:
- < 1 year
- 1 < 2 years
- 2 < 4 years
- 4 < 5 years
- > 5 years

Values on chart: 6, 4, 4, 5, 9

Source of data: Mediation research project national survey of Community Mediation Services

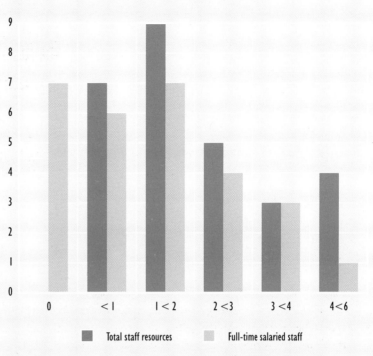

Figure 4.2: Total staffing resources including volunteers.

Total staff resources ■   Full-time salaried staff ▢

Source of data: Mediation research project national survey of Community Mediation Services

Size of community mediation services

Community mediation services vary considerably in the number and composition of their staff. Some services rely entirely on volunteers to undertake all functions, including that of co-ordinator. Others employ one or more paid staff (normally a co-ordinator, but sometimes also one or more administrators) while relying on volunteer mediators. In some services mediators are also paid, sometimes on a sessional basis (amounting to more than just expenses but not full pay), and sometimes on full pay, either for all or part of a week.

Figure 4.2 shows how mediation services compare, both in terms of the total staffing resources available to them (including volunteers),[3] and also the number of salaried staff they employ.[4]

As can be seen, only four services had more than four full-time staff equivalents working for them (in whatever capacity), and seven services had fewer than one FTE. As for paid staff, only four services had three or more full-time salaried staff, and seven had no paid staff at all. We will deal with the issue of financial resources and funding arrangements at the end of this chapter.

Range of mediation services offered and types of neighbour disputes dealt with

All the Community Mediation Services in the sample offered mediation for neighbour disputes, and for most of them this constituted the single biggest category of work by far.[5] A number of the services that responded to the survey also referred to other mediation services on offer. They included the resolution of family conflicts (mentioned by 9 services); noise complaints other than neighbour noise (mentioned by 8 services); conflict resolution in schools (mentioned by 6 services); commercial mediation and victim offender mediation (each mentioned by 3 services); domestic violence, employment and debt management (each mentioned by 1 service). However, in most cases these other forms of

mediation comprised a very small proportion of their total workload. There was only one service[6] in which the proportion of neighbour disputes dealt with fell below 50%.

As for the type of neighbour disputes referred, 21 of the services provided us with information, which is set out in Figure 4.3. As can be seen, the breakdown is broadly comparable with the type of neighbour disputes that are referred to local authority housing service departments (see Figure 2.3). Once again, disputes about noise predominate and account for 42% of all neighbour dispute referrals. Between them, disputes over noise, boundaries, inter-personal conflict and children account for 70% of all disputes referred.[7]

Very little change was reported in the pattern of dispute types referred, which is not surprising given the relatively recent emergence of most of the services, but two of the longer-established services reported that there had been an increase in the proportion of disputes relating to noise, and two reported that the number of cases involving anti-social behaviour or harassment had increased. Two services described seasonal variations in the pattern of referrals, with an increase in 'noise' cases in winter, while boundary disputes and complaints relating to children were more commonplace in summer.

No fewer than 21 of the services indicated that they were hoping or planning to expand the range of mediation services on offer. Almost half of these (10) mentioned conflict resolution in schools, five referred to commercial mediation, four referred to victim offender mediation and both family mediation and elder or inter-generational mediation were

LIVERPOOL JOHN MOORES UNIVERSITY
LEARNING SERVICES

Figure 4.3: Type of neighbour disputes referred to community mediation services.

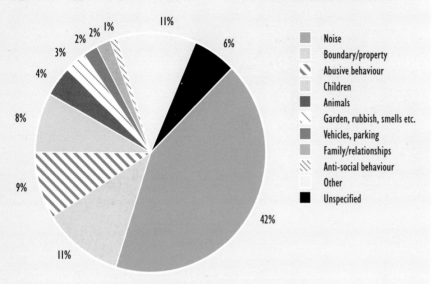

Source of data: Mediation research project national survey of Community Mediation Services

received from different sources, some receiving very few referrals from a particular source while others received the lion's share of their referrals from that same source.

Relations with referral agencies and satisfaction with referral rates

In general, mediation services appear to enjoy good relations with their referral agencies,[10] though four services indicated that they had better relations with some agencies than with others. When asked whether they received as many referrals from each of their main referrals organisations as they might, however, the responses were rather less positive. Only four services expressed complete satisfaction with the number of referrals they received. As many as three quarters of the services (23) indicated that they would like to receive more referrals, though seven of these explained that they were unable to take on more at the present time, either because they lacked the resources or because they did not wish to expand too rapidly. Eight other services attributed the low referral rate to the fact that they had not been operational for very long, and had not yet had time to develop a close relationship with their main referral organisations or demonstrate their potential.

also referred to by three services. At present, however, it appears that the great majority of community mediation services specialise almost exclusively in providing mediation in relation to neighbour disputes.

Source of referrals to community mediation services

Twenty five community mediation services provided detailed information about their sources of referrals, and the averages obtained are shown in Figure 4.4.

As can be seen, the biggest category comprises 'self-referrals',[8] which account for just over one in five of all neighbour dispute referrals. The proportion of referrals made by housing departments and environmental health services is relatively small[9] (19% and 6% respectively), though this is again in line with the findings from our general survey of local authority housing and environmental health service departments since only a small proportion of cases were dealt with by referring them for mediation. Other voluntary advice agencies accounted for more than one in six referrals where the source was specified, and the police were responsible for more than one in ten of all referrals.

However, individual services differed quite considerably in the proportion of referrals they

Eight of the services expressing disappointment at the low referral rate felt that the problem lay with the referral agencies themselves. Four services took the view that staff in the referring organisations were insufficiently aware of the service or its benefits. One problem referred to was the difficulty some of them had finding the time to build and maintain relationships with referral agencies; another was the problem of staff turnover in the referring agencies. Finally, a further four services felt they did not receive a sufficient number of referrals, either because staff in referring organisations see dealing with neighbour disputes as their own job or they feel that their own service is adequate. The general impression conveyed is that several community mediation services could take on more neighbour dispute referrals than they currently receive, and most expect to be able to take on more referrals in the future. If this is to happen, however, staff in referral agencies will need to be convinced that mediation is an appropriate way of dealing with at least some of the neighbour dispute cases they are called upon to deal with.

Number of referrals and proportion of cases accepted for mediation

Twenty five mediation services were able to provide us with information on the number of cases referred to the service, though only 20 services provided us with referral figures over a twelve-month period as requested. The total number of cases referred to these 20 services was 2652, which averages out at around 133 referrals per service. The minimum number of referrals received by a service over the twelve month period was 22; the maximum was 310. By extrapolating the figures provided by the five services which provided returns relating to a

Figure 4.4: Source of referrals.

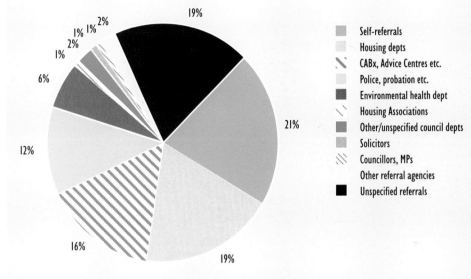

Source of data: Mediation research project national survey of Community Mediation Services

longer or shorter period it is possible to estimate the combined number of referrals over a twelve month period for all the services supplying data. When this is done, the revised total number of referrals is 2,928, with an average of 113 per service. Figure 4.5 shows the number of referrals per service on this basis.

Considering only the more established services, which had been running for a period of two or more years,[11] 13 of which provided referral data for the period requested, the total number of cases referred was 1,923. The average number of cases referred to these established services was 148, with a minimum of 26 and a maximum of 310.

Twenty two services were able to provide us with figures showing both the number of cases referred, and the number that were accepted in relation to the same time period. The average proportion of referred cases that were accepted by all these services was just under 80%, and ranged from 35% (Dorset) to 100% (6 services). For the more established services,[12] the

Figure 4.5: Number of referrals per service.

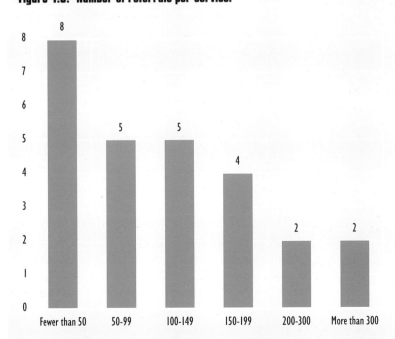

Source of data: Mediation research project national survey of Community Mediation Services

average acceptance rate was just over three quarters (76%), ranging from 55% (Bristol) to 100% (Coventry and Milton Keynes). The completion rate for the ten established services for which we had the data was 96% of all accepted cases, and 78.5% of all referrals.

Criteria for accepting cases

Unlike local authority housing departments, community mediation services do not differentiate between the types of tenure that might be involved when considering whether or not to accept referrals. Nor is it necessary for a complainant to establish that the behaviour complained of constitutes either a statutory nuisance or a breach of a tenancy condition. Potentially, therefore, community mediation services would appear to be very much less restrictive than either local authority housing or environmental health service departments in the range of neighbour disputes they may be willing to take on.

Most services do nevertheless have a list of criteria (or at least considerations) that help them to decide whether or not to become involved in a particular dispute.[13] But because they are mainly independent organisations, and operate according to their own guidelines, there is little uniformity in the criteria they employ, which makes it difficult to generalise.

The most frequently mentioned criterion is a willingness to participate in the process and acceptance of the principles of mediation. This was mentioned by eighteen of the services responding to our survey. Half of these stipulate that the first party at least should be willing to participate or at least accept the principles of mediation. The other half require both parties to be willing to participate. This is understandable, since mediation is best thought of as a voluntary process, but it does mean that many cases that might in other respects have been suitable for mediation will have to be turned down on this ground.

Just over one quarter of the services (8) operate with an explicit geographical criterion, and require one party (or in some cases both) to reside within a particular district. Five services stipulate that it has to be a dispute involving neighbours or near residents (as opposed to some other type of dispute e.g. family). Four services said they would not accept cases with court proceedings or legal action in process.

Five services do not accept cases involving people with a history of violence or threats of violence or a risk to the mediators. Two services tend not to accept cases involving racial harassment. Three services take mental health factors into consideration, and one indicated that it rejected cases where 'psychotic mental illness' is a factor. Two services reject cases where there is a power imbalance and two services referred explicitly to the possibility that cases might have to be turned away when the service is overloaded or lacks the resources to take on a particular case. In addition, we came across a number of other services that also appear in practice to 'ration' the service that is provided in this way (or by operating a 'de facto' waiting list), suggesting that the practice may be more widespread. The criteria employed by individual services are outlined in Appendix 1.

How neighbour disputes are dealt with by Community Mediation Services

The process of mediation has been described elsewhere (see, for example, Mediation UK, 1993: p.6; Karn et al., 1993: ch. 5) and can take various forms. The aim of the process is to enable the parties to a dispute to reach a mutually acceptable resolution of the issues for themselves, rather than having one imposed on them by any outside body or agency. The main strategies used to facilitate this outcome involve direct or 'face to face' mediation; indirect mediation (sometimes known as 'shuttle diplomacy'); and work with one party.

Direct mediation involves both (or all) parties in a meeting that is arranged and facilitated by the mediator(s) at a neutral venue. The mediator's role is to help to define the issues and also the common ground between the parties, and to encourage them to exchange views and feelings, and then negotiate a mutually agreeable solution to the conflict. Where the parties refuse to meet face to face the mediator may still be able to act as a 'go-between' and, by conveying messages and responses between the parties, facilitate the process of exchange and negotiation.

In some cases one of the parties may not wish to get involved in the process of mediation.

Sometimes the party initiating contact with the mediation service may not wish the matter to be taken any further. Although more limited, the mediator may still have a constructive role to play in such cases by suggesting or exploring ways of resolving or at least handling the conflict without any need for third-party intervention. The situation may be more difficult where the 'other' party refuses to have anything to do with the process, but even here it may sometimes be helpful for the 'first' party to be able to discuss with the mediator possible forms of non-confrontational 'unilateral' action that might help to defuse or resolve a conflict.

Figure 4.6 shows the proportion of cases dealt with by each of these three main approaches. Just under half of all cases involved a process of indirect mediation, while just over one quarter resulted in direct mediation and a similar proportion involved working with just a single party.

Virtually all the mediation services participating in the survey indicated that mediators worked in pairs when attempting to mediate between parties once a case has been accepted.[14] Likewise, in the great majority of services (21) it is usual for mediators to work in pairs when assessing the suitability of referrals. Only five services indicated that mediators work singly for this purpose, while two services had no set policy and a further three did not indicate what their policy was.

Whatever strategies are adopted by community mediation services in seeking to resolve a dispute, there are a number of important differences between the process of mediation and conventional responses to the problem. One of the main differences is one of perception regarding the very nature of neighbour disputes themselves.

Mediation seeks to be non-judgmental in its approach, and this is symbolised in its rejection of the terms 'complainant' and 'alleged perpetrator'. The refusal to adopt such adversarial terminology is not simply an acknowledgement that there may be two sides to most disputes, but also reflects a recognition that even where one party appears to be acting totally unreasonably this may be symptomatic of more fundamental problems that may need to be addressed if harmony is to be restored. Disputes, in

other words, are often not what they seem, and for mediators the behaviour giving rise to them may frequently be considered to be symptomatic of 'the real problem' rather than its cause.

The process of mediation is also distinctive in seeking to vest control over, and responsibility for, the dispute firmly in the hands of the parties themselves. In contrast with most other agencies, mediation does not require the parties to a dispute to couch their problem within a particular conceptual or linguistic framework; nor are they required to focus

Figure 4.6: How cases were dealt with by mediation services.

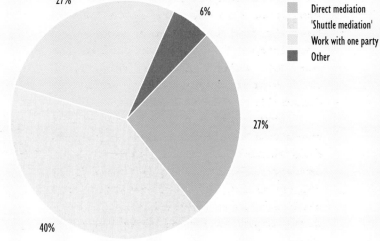

Source of data: Mediation research project national survey of Community Mediation Services

only on certain selected aspects of the conflict to the exclusion of others, as is often the case in a court of law.

This difference in approach between mediation services and that of most other agencies called upon to deal with neighbour disputes is also reflected in an ongoing debate within the mediation movement itself over the main aims of mediation and the way 'success' should be defined.[15] For some in the mediation movement, the primary aim of the process is to help parties talk through their differences with a view to securing either a formal or informal agreement that both (or all) can live with. Others are more interested in the achievement of greater understanding between disputants, and fostering attitudes and skills that will help disputants to resolve future disputes themselves.

Figure 4.7: Case outcomes as recorded by mediation services.

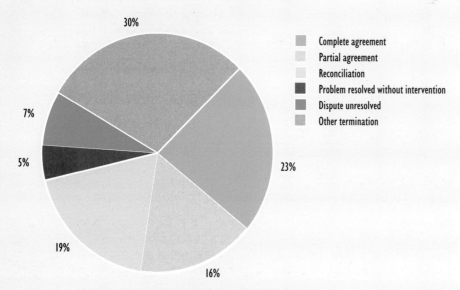

Complete agreement
Partial agreement
Reconciliation
Problem resolved without intervention
Dispute unresolved
Other termination

30%
7%
5%
19%
16%
23%

Source of data: Mediation research project national survey of Community Mediation Services

reached. Almost one in five cases were said to have resulted in some measure of reconciliation or improved understanding between the parties without there being a formal agreement. Only 7% of cases were categorised as 'unresolved' because of irreconcilable differences remaining between the parties. However, almost one in three cases terminated for other reasons, usually because one of the parties was unwilling to participate or to proceed further with the mediation. We will return to this issue when comparing the quality and costs of mediation and conventional methods of dealing with neighbour disputes in Chapter 9.

This debate is sometimes characterised as a contest between 'satisfaction-based aims' which emphasise the importance of 'formal outcomes' and 'transformationist aims' which lay greater stress on conflict-resolving processes and attitudes.[16] For present purposes, the most significant aspect of the debate is that it emphasises still further the difficulty of comparing mediation with conventional ways of dealing with neighbour disputes since they differ fundamentally not only in their approach but also in their basic aspirations and objectives.

Reported outcomes for neighbour disputes dealt with by mediation

We asked all respondents to classify the outcome of their completed cases, and the responses we received are shown in Figure 4.7. In terms of the 'satisfaction versus transformation' debate which we referred to above, the first two outcomes (complete or partial agreement) reflect a satisfaction-based goal while 'reconciliation' (which may also be complete or partial) is more consistent with a transformation-based goal.

On the basis of these self assessments,[17] almost one in four cases were said to have resulted in complete agreement on all issues, and a further 16% of cases concluded in a partial agreement being

Financial resources and funding arrangements

Community mediation services vary considerably with regard to both the sources and scale of their funding. Figure 4.8 shows the range and distribution of funds received by the 28 services that provided us with the financial information we requested.[18] In most cases the information provided was for the most recent twelve month period available at the time of the survey.[19]

As can be seen, incomes ranged from under £1,000 to over £60,000, though no service had an income in excess of £80,000. It should be remembered, also, that some of the smaller services depend heavily on the time given freely by volunteer mediators, co-ordinators, administrators or development workers.

The main sources of funding are shown in Figure 4.9.[20] The biggest source of funding comprises borough, city and county councils, which contribute just over 40% (equivalent to £271,357) of the total funds received by community mediation services, and nineteen of the 29 services for which we obtained information received funding from this source.

The amounts involved, and the numbers of

Figure 4.8: Funds received by mediation services.

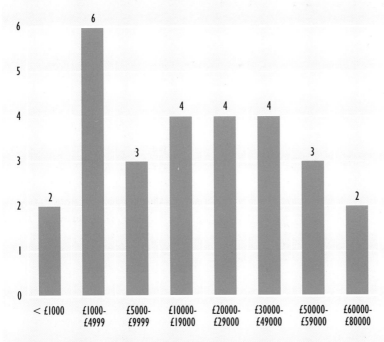

Source of data: Mediation research project national survey of Community Mediation Services

66% of the total) was the bill for salaries and associated expenditure. Twenty services incurred costs under this heading, the amounts ranging from under £1,000 to over £20,000. However, this does not represent the true 'cost' of the professional services provided, since many of these are volunteered.

The same is also true of other 'costs', such as rent and rates (representing 6% of the total expenditure), since only 17 services pay rent, even though every service makes use of premises. In many cases the donation of rent-free premises represents a contribution in kind. Likewise, only eight services indicated that they incurred significant expenditure on service costs such as cleaning and maintenance or charges for utilities, which suggests that these could also represent hidden subsidies. However, such unquantified 'resource costs' do pose problems (as we shall see) when seeking to compare the cost-effectiveness of community mediation services with public agencies that do incur these charges.

Another significant item of expenditure

services in receipt of each of the main sources of funding are shown in Figure 4.10. National charities and central government grants each provide 17% of the total (£112,210 and £107,165) respectively, but are more likely to be concentrated in larger amounts, benefiting fewer services. The same is also true of Safer Cities funding (which represents 6% of the total), which is also provided by central government.

Local charities and industry/commerce are also important but relatively minor sources of income, and the amounts obtained from these sources are often considerably smaller.

Expenditure and community mediation service budgets

Not surprisingly, the budgets and levels of expenditure incurred by community mediation service are determined very largely by their income levels. Figure 4.11 shows a break-down of the total amount spent by the 27 community mediation services providing information on expenditure.

Figure 4.12 shows the range of expenditure incurred by the 27 services providing information on expenditure in respect of the main budget headings. Of the total expenditure of £590,882 by far the biggest amount (representing

Figure 4.9: Current main funding sources for mediation services.

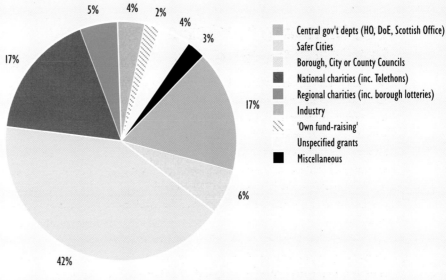

Source of data: Mediation research project national survey of Community Mediation Services

Figure 4.10: Distribution of funding to individual mediation services.

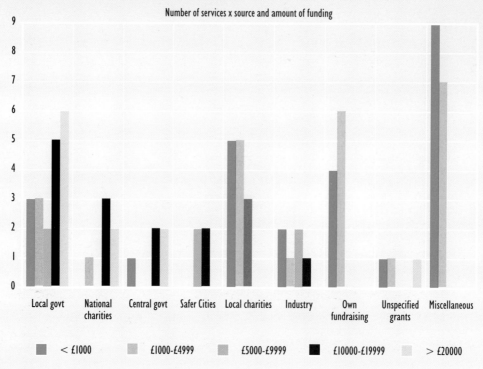

Number of services x source and amount of funding

Source of data: Mediation research project national survey of Community Mediation Services

(accounting for 7% of the total) comprises the bill for recruitment and training. No fewer than twenty three services incurred costs under this heading (ranging from less than £100 to upwards of £5,000 in a twelve month period). The other main items of expenditure include stationery and travel costs (accounting for 4.9% and 4.7% of the total respectively).

Concerns over fund-raising and resource issues

Although some individual mediation services have shown themselves to be adept at both direct fund-raising and 'creative resourcing', there is no doubt that funding represents one of the biggest challenges and problems confronting mediation services in general. Several indicated that insecurity of funding made planning difficult.

Another related problem is that the need to expend much time and effort on fund raising can leave little time for actually delivering the service. Moreover, some services find it difficult to obtain, train and then keep good committed volunteers, many of whom are looking to gain relevant experience before obtaining paid work in the field. In addition, staff shortages often mean that people have to be 'jacks of all trades', and there are problems of juggling various responsibilities – for example balancing increasing demands for training and consultancy (or other forms of fund-raising) against actually providing a mediation service. In particular, it may be difficult to find appropriate mediators for specific cases, and one or two services indicated that otherwise suitable referrals may have to be rejected for this reason.

Growing and developing can

Figure 4.11: Main items of expenditure incurred by mediation services.

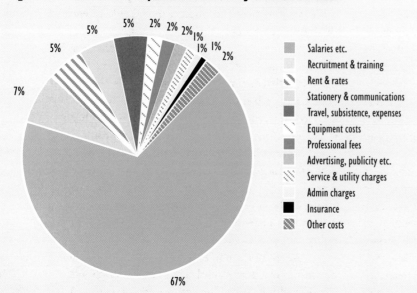

Salaries etc.
Recruitment & training
Rent & rates
Stationery & communications
Travel, subsistence, expenses
Equipment costs
Professional fees
Advertising, publicity etc.
Service & utility charges
Admin charges
Insurance
Other costs

Source of data: Mediation research project national survey of Community Mediation Services

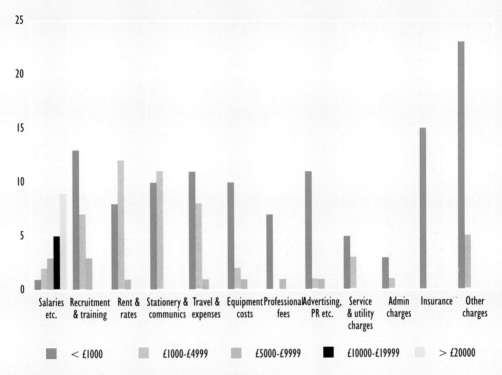

Figure 4.12: Break-down of expenditure for community mediation services showing items and amounts involved.

Legend: ▮ < £1000 ▮ £1000-£4999 ▮ £5000-£9999 ▮ £10000-£19999 ▮ > £20000

Source of data: Mediation research project national survey of Community Mediation Services

also be a bit of a 'chicken and egg' problem. Services can't take on too many cases until they are ready but, in order to grow, they need to take on more cases. Managing this transition is likely to be extremely difficult, and may be made worse if at the same time trying to recruit, train and organise a panel of volunteers. We came across a number of instances in which services resorted to formal or informal waiting lists in an effort to cope, but the danger here is that potential referrers who become aware of the problem may become reluctant to refer suitable cases to the service. Once again, this point was made to us by otherwise sympathetic local government officers who felt inhibited about using their local mediation service because of such resource constraints.

A somewhat different source of anxiety over funding, but one that is familiar to many with experience of the voluntary sector, is the concern that the service may come to be directed more by funding opportunities rather than by need. Similarly, there were concerns that if services didn't attain their core funding targets, other extensions of the service, and possibly even its main function would falter and maybe even fail.

Even services that had managed to negotiate 'secure' sources of funding expressed anxieties over this issue. For example, a number of services have managed to negotiate 'service level agreements' with their local housing or environmental health service departments whereby, in return for a 'block grant', they agree to accept a given number of referrals. However, some of these services expressed concern over their ability to provide a service to those resi-

dents who are not covered by the contracts. In addition, problems can also be caused when other organisations that are not parties to the agreement (such as a local housing association) also refer large numbers of cases to a mediation service whose main source of funding is provided by the local authority's housing or environmental health department.

Finally, other worries revolved around the use of volunteers. Some services felt that they may have to start paying some volunteers in order to keep them, but this raises the problem of paying some volunteers and not others. There were also worries that moving from volunteers to paid staff may damage the ethos of the service. Other potential conflicts revolved around whether services should move into new areas and whether they should extend their geographic area.

On the whole, potential conflicts would seem to stem from the effort of trying to do as much as possible with a minimal amount of resources, thereby raising the problem of whether resources should be directed towards one area rather than another. Concerns relating to the issue of funding predominated in response to questions both about the main problems encountered by service co-ordinators to date, and also about possible conflicts of objective arising in the future. Consequently, this is an issue we will return to later in the report when addressing the policy implications raised by the research.

Apart from funding, one concern expressed by some of the more recently established services was the difficulty of becoming known and accepted. A couple of services mentioned the more specific problems of covering a large rural area. In a slightly different vein, some mentioned the problem of obtaining cases later rather than sooner, by which time the prospects for successful mediation may have substantially diminished. We return to some of these issues in Chapter 10.

Notes

1   On the process of mediation, and how it works in practice, see Mediation UK (1993); Karn et al. (1993).

2   Only three of these were involved in victim offender resolution as well as providing a mediation service for neighbour disputes.

3   Which is expressed in terms of full-time staff equivalents. When analysing the returns, thirty five hours of volunteer time per week was taken as the equivalent of one full time paid member of staff.

4   Figures relate only to staff dealing with neighbour disputes. In two services which also undertake victim offender mediation, an appropriate deduction was made, to exclude staff not involved with neighbour dispute mediation.

5   Over half the services (17) indicated that more than 90% of their work consisted of neighbour dispute mediation, while a further nine said that it was by far the biggest category of work without giving precise figures. In only two services did the proportion of community mediation undertaken fall to 50% or less of the total.

6   Mediation Dorset, where the proportion of neighbour disputes was 40%, which was equalled only by family conflict work.

7   The category labelled 'other' in Figure 4.3 includes those disputes classified as 'other' or 'miscellaneous' by the services themselves, and also any categories of dispute that appeared only once or very infrequently across the sample. The category labelled 'unspecified' represents the proportion of disputes that was not separately itemised, since some services only included their major dispute categories.

8   Defined as those cases which 'are not referred or directed to the service by some other agency'.

9   One service gave figures only for their main referral source (self-referrals), leaving the others unspecified, so the actual proportion of cases coming from these two sources is probably slightly higher than indicated, though still relatively modest.

10 Sixteen services described these as 'excellent' or 'very good'; 7 described them as being 'good'; and a further three described them as 'satisfactory'.

11 Excluding MESH, in Sheffield, which at the time of the survey had recently been relaunched on a different basis.

12 Defined as those which had been in continuous operation for a period of two years or more. Of the fifteen services within this category twelve provided us with information relating to both referrals and accepted cases during the period we requested.

13 But not all do. Some of the smaller and most recently established services, have not yet articulated a set of criteria and, at the time of the survey, had accepted all referrals received so far. One of the longer-established services, Lambeth, appears to operate an ad hoc policy of discussing potentially difficult cases on their own merits.

14 Only one of the 29 services that responded to this question indicated that mediators worked singly on accepted cases, and two services did not disclose their policy.

15 We discuss this further in an unpublished report (Dignan and Sorsby, 1995) that was produced as part of a project to develop a national database for use by community mediation services. Although part of the current research project, this aspect was a relatively self-contained element, and has therefore been written up separately.

16 See Bush and Folger (1994: Chapter 1) for further discussion, and Acland (1995: 8-9) for a useful summary of the different strands within the debate.

17 Unfortunately, it was beyond the scope of the present project to obtain the views of the parties themselves, though a comparative consumer satisfaction survey involving disputants whose disputes had been handled by means of the different agencies/approaches would provide a very useful follow-up to the present study.

18 The Figure shows the total funds received by each service during the most recent 12-month period for which data was available, with the exception of services (e.g. Plymouth and Coventry) that also provided victim/ offender mediation. Here, only the proportion of funding that is attributable to their neighbour dispute work is shown.

19 Unfortunately, not all services were able to provide data for the same period. The earliest period was April 1993 - March 1994. The most recent was April 1995 to March 1996 (partly prospective). In addition, three of the services provided us with information relating to a period other than twelve months (Brighton Mediation 13 months, Camden Mediation Service 11 months and Worthing and District Mediation Service 6 months).

20 Once again, the figures provide only an approximation since, as we have indicated previously, the funding periods are not the same for each of the community mediation services.

Assessing the human and economic costs of neighbour disputes on the parties themselves

Assessing the scale of the problem: media reports and existing statistics

Giant conifers[1] ... Corky the cockerel[2] .... Flossie, the Vietnamese pot-bellied pig[3] .... the phantom pond-slasher[4]'. Neighbour disputes make good newspaper copy, and are often used to portray the quirkier side of human nature, as the above headlines illustrate. However, there is also a darker side, since the effects on those involved can often be devastating, blighting their lives for years on end.

In a recent feud over a conifer hedge, for example, which was widely reported in the national press, the dispute lasted for 18 years and was estimated to have cost £100,000 in court and legal fees. For some, the consequences can be even more tragic, and one newspaper report documented seventeen fatalities involving neighbourhood noise over a six year period up to December 1994.[5] A content analysis survey of the Times newspaper conducted as part of the present study produced four reports of fatalities resulting from disputes between neighbours during the first eight months of 1996 alone.

As for the impact of neighbour disputes on the parties themselves, the only national statistics of which we are aware relate to the 1991 national noise survey (the BRE study). This contains information about the way people are affected by neighbour noise from various sources, and some of the main findings are summarised in Table 5.1.

From this, it will be seen that the sources of neighbour noise to which respondents were most likely to object were barking dogs closely followed by door banging, radio/TV/Hi-fi. Very high proportions of those who heard the various forms of neighbour noise claimed to be irritated or disturbed by it and between one-half and three-quarters of all who heard noise from the various sources considered them to be a nuisance to them personally.

Beyond such bland statistics, it is almost impossible to quantify the adverse impact that neighbour disputes undoubtedly have on those most directly affected, since the kind of data that would be required is not currently collected by any of the agencies responsible for dealing with neighbour disputes, and to undertake a reliable and systematic examination of all the costs involved would be a major project in its own right, even for a limited sample of disputants. Instead, we have adopted a more qualitative approach, in which we first identify the type of costs that might be involved, and then

Table 5.1: Numbers affected by neighbour noise and its effects on those who heard it.

Source of noise	Number who[1] heard noise	Percentage affected who:				
		Objected to noise	Were irritated by noise	Were disturbed by it at times	Were annoyed by it at times	Considered noise a nuisance
Barking dogs	186	80	93	86	76	70
Doors banging	104	75	88	90	66	74
Radio/TV/Hi-fi	184	73	87	85	73	70
Peoples voices	235	71	87	92	70	69
Children	195	68	81	90	74	69
Cars/m'cycles	131	67	88	89	69	72
DIY	108	58	83	83	59	61
Vacuum cleaners	50	55	85	85	70	65
Footsteps	50	54	69	96	54	50
Lawn mowers	100	45	77	71	39	58

[1] Actual number of respondents who heard noise from this source, from a total number of 2,373

Source of data: Building Research Establishment National Noise Attitude Survey (Department of the Environment, 1966, Table 6.1)

LIVERPOOL JOHN MOORES UNIVERSITY
LEARNING SERVICES

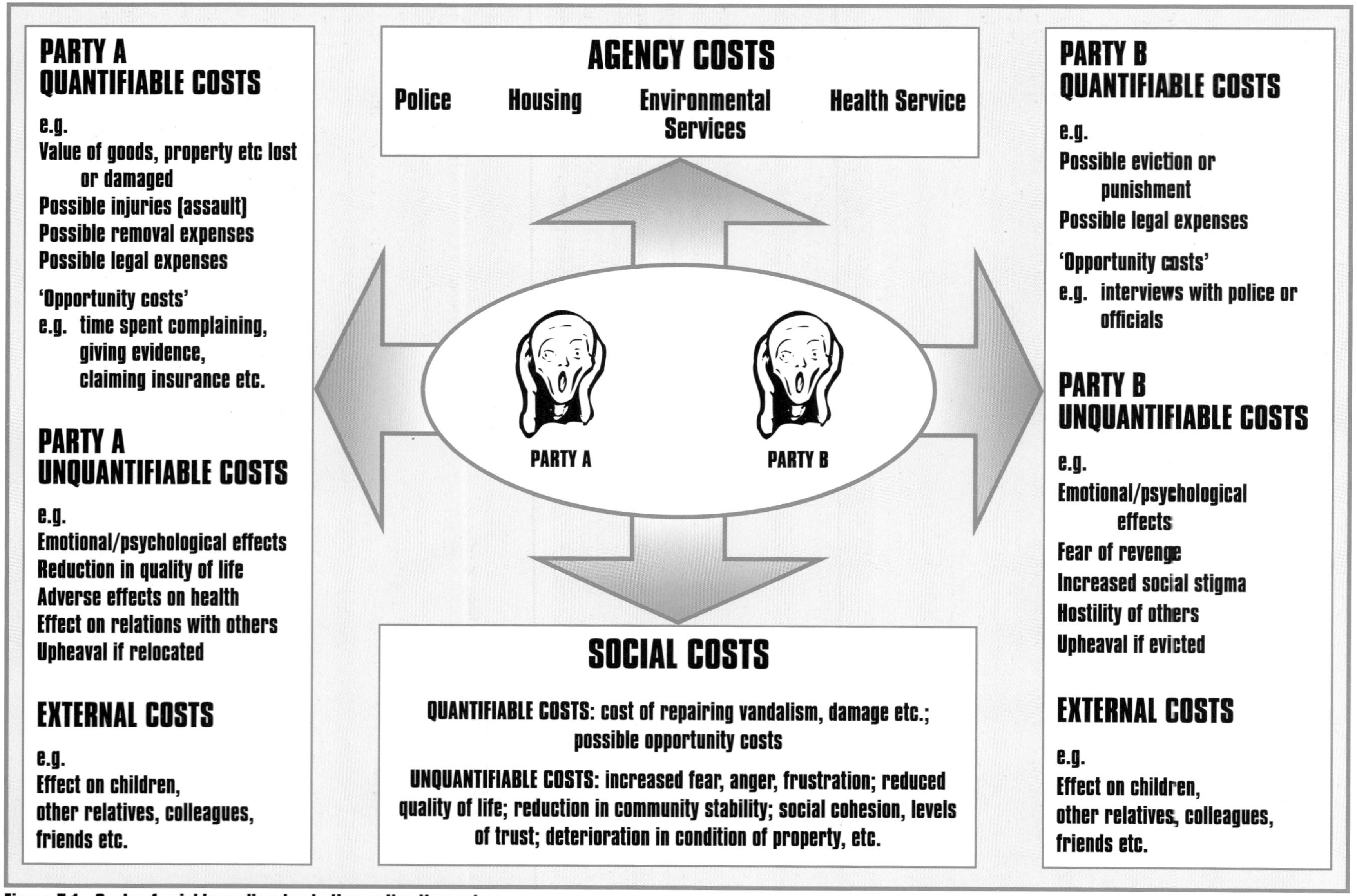

AGENCY COSTS

Police Housing Environmental Services Health Service

PARTY A

PARTY B

PARTY A
QUANTIFIABLE COSTS

e.g.
Value of goods, property etc lost or damaged
Possible injuries (assault)
Possible removal expenses
Possible legal expenses

'Opportunity costs'
e.g. time spent complaining, giving evidence, claiming insurance etc.

PARTY A
UNQUANTIFIABLE COSTS

e.g.
Emotional/psychological effects
Reduction in quality of life
Adverse effects on health
Effect on relations with others
Upheaval if relocated

EXTERNAL COSTS

e.g.
Effect on children,
other relatives, colleagues,
friends etc.

PARTY B
QUANTIFIABLE COSTS

e.g.
Possible eviction or punishment
Possible legal expenses

'Opportunity costs'
e.g. interviews with police or officials

PARTY B
UNQUANTIFIABLE COSTS

e.g.
Emotional/psychological effects
Fear of revenge
Increased social stigma
Hostility of others
Upheaval if evicted

EXTERNAL COSTS

e.g.
Effect on children,
other relatives, colleagues,
friends etc.

SOCIAL COSTS

QUANTIFIABLE COSTS: cost of repairing vandalism, damage etc.; possible opportunity costs

UNQUANTIFIABLE COSTS: increased fear, anger, frustration; reduced quality of life; reduction in community stability; social cohesion, levels of trust; deterioration in condition of property, etc.

Figure 5.1: Costs of neighbour disputes to the parties themselves.

seek to illustrate these with reference to a number of case histories which we have drawn from a variety of sources.

Identifying the type of costs involved

Disputes between neighbours are likely to impose a variety of human and economic costs, both on the parties themselves, and also the agencies having to deal with them, though very little research on this has been undertaken to date. In Figure 5.1 we have tried to identify some of the main inter-party (and wider social) costs that might be involved in neighbour disputes, though even this is not exhaustive.

Many of the direct financial costs for the parties concerned could in principle be quantified, but since even these are likely to vary considerably from case to case, generalisations are difficult if not impossible to make. Similarly, it would be possible, though less straightforward, to calculate the 'opportunity costs' that are involved in making complaints, giving evidence or replacing lost or damaged items. Other costs, such as the personal and emotional costs to the parties and their families, are much more difficult to quantify. Given the almost infinite variety in the nature and scale of neighbour disputes, however, it may be more illuminating to try to illustrate some of the costs that can be incurred as a result of neighbour disputes with reference to individual case histories.

Cases illustrating the human costs of neighbour disputes

The first four cases illustrate the potentially devastating consequences that may arise when neighbour disputes get out of hand, and were all widely reported in the national press while the current project was under way.[6]

Case history 1[7]

In July 1994, an irate neighbour was so incensed by the noise of a pay party taking place four floors above his own ninth storey flat that he hurled a petrol bomb into the hall-way, resulting in the death of one of the party-goers who fell from the balcony. The neighbour was convicted of murder, but the judge strongly criticised the council for

failing to prevent the noise pollution, and said that they should bear some of the moral responsibility for the tragedy which ensued.

Case history 2[8]

In February 1996 a rock fan was convicted of manslaughter and jailed for five years after stabbing to death a neighbour who complained about Led Zeppelin music being played at full volume.

Case history 3[9]

In March 1996 a man pleaded guilty to manslaughter after hitting his neighbour on the head with a crowbar during an altercation over the neighbour's persistently barking puppy.

Case history 4[10]

In August 1996 a man died after a fight which started when a group of local youths were heard threatening his two pot-bellied piglets. Eighteen months earlier another pot-bellied pig he was rearing had been killed by rat poison.

Even in cases that do not hit the headlines, the effect that anti-social behaviour can have on neighbours is often traumatic, as the next two examples illustrate.[11] They also highlight the important point we made earlier (see page 33) about the impossibility of quantifying some of the human and social costs that are incurred as a result of some of the more intractable neighbour disputes.

Case history 5

Starting in April 1995, Housing Department officials in one urban local authority[12] received a series of complaints from residents about the behaviour of one of their neighbours in a low rise block of flats. He was alleged to have repeatedly disrupted his neighbours' water supply – on one occasion by sawing through the water pipe, which caused flooding to the flat immediately downstairs. The downstairs neighbour also complained that his telephone cable had been cut, and the door intercom damaged. On another occasion the tenant in question was believed to have damaged the main electrical fuses for the flats which, in the opinion of the electrician who was called out, presented a fire hazard and was extremely dangerous for all the residents.

LIVERPOOL JOHN MOORES UNIVERSITY
LEARNING SERVICES

Another neighbour, who was accused by the allegedly anti-social tenant of trying to break into his flat, found that the wheel nuts on his van had been loosened and a substance, which could have been white spirit, was poured through his letter box. A few days later lighted paper was pushed through his letter box, and a week later a bag with the words 'bomb bag' written on it were stuck onto his door. This neighbour was reported to be afraid of leaving his flat empty. Several of the residents complained that their neighbour had damaged their cars and hit their front doors with a hammer.

The relevant housing file contained a total of 82 entries relating to a twelve-month period between 4 April 1995 and 29 March 1996. Among the many letters received by housing officers one complainant spoke of his health being adversely affected by the anti-social behaviour, and of the distress which it caused to himself and other residents in the block. The downstairs neighbour also wrote to the Director of Housing complaining of depression. Subsequently, the police expressed concern for the latter's safety and informed the housing office that in their view he had been subjected to excessive nuisance from his anti-social neighbour. A letter from the Police Superintendent reported fourteen incidents at which the police were required to attend in relation to this particular tenant.

Case history 6

In another neighbour dispute case brought about by mental health problems, Housing Department officials in a different area of the same urban local authority began receiving complaints in February 1991 about banging doors and excessively loud music being played (between midnight and 5.30 am). The tenant whose behaviour was the subject of complaint (Tenant A) was a man of 30 years of age who lived alone in a one-bedroomed flat which he had occupied since December 1988. Tenant A appeared to be suffering from a form of schizophrenia, and also had a serious alcohol problem. Over the next 2 years A's behaviour deteriorated steadily, and a catalogue of complaints built up alleging noise, abuse and various acts of anti-social behaviour from a total of ten neighbouring tenants.[13]

In one incident he kicked in the door of a

neighbouring flat in the early hours of the morning and threatened the female tenant (Tenant C) in her bedroom. The police arrested Tenant A and released him on bail. In December 1993 Tenant A was sectioned and spent six weeks in hospital. Six months later the police were called after Tenant A broke one of his neighbour's windows with a hammer. In July 1995 Tenant A was sectioned again, but absconded and assaulted neighbouring Tenant (G) on his return to the flats. Although picked up by the police and returned to the hospital, he again absconded for a short while, and was eventually persuaded to accept rehousing on being released from hospital in the autumn of 1995. Meanwhile, the Department indicated that it would be attempting to clean Tenant A's flat out as it was a potential health hazard.

Tenant A's new flat was on the sixth floor of a recently refurbished multi-storey block of flats. In January 1996, housing officers received a telephone complaint alleging noise nuisance from one of Tenant A's new neighbours, Tenant K. Over the next three months similar complaints were made by three other neighbours. While investigating these on 11 April, housing officers reported that Tenant A appeared to have had a small fire in the kitchen. He himself was reported to be lucid and polite.

On 16 April 1996 reports were received that the previous evening Tenant A had turned all his taps on, resulting in flooding to all the flats below his own. The police attended and had to break down the door to gain admission. It was later suggested that Tenant A's actions might have been a response to his belief that the basement was inhabited by a demon spirit.

As a result of the flooding, a number of tenants in the adjoining properties had no electricity, and several had to dispose of the entire contents of their deep-freezers. All the carpets were soaked. One neighbour had had to seek alternative accommodation for one night because of the lack of electricity. The cost of repairing the damage to the flat door, rewiring, lift repairs and electricity board charges was estimated at £2,100, excluding compensation to neighbours and any insurance pay-outs. Tenant A was admitted to hospital, and was advised for his own safety that it would be unwise for him to return to his flat unattended as several of his neighbours were extremely angry.

[Despite this advice, he did subsequently return]. One week after the incident Tenant A's flat was found to be infested with maggots and flies, and had to be disinfested.

The relevant housing file contained a total of separate 221 entries for the period 22 February 1991 to 16 July 1996, by which date it was still ongoing. During this period no fewer than 88 complaints had been logged, from a total of 17 separate complainants (10 in the original property and 7 in the new premises). The number of complaints made by each tenant ranged from one (from each of 7 tenants) to 28 (in respect of Tenant G). However, Tenant A had also issued 15 complaints, nine relating to a dog owned by Tenant G and two against Tenant D.

Quite apart from the physical assaults and severe damage caused by Tenant A to the property of both the council and his neighbouring residents, the file also contained a number of reports expressing concern at the effect which his behaviour and the dispute were having on various of the other residents.

One of these (Tenant G) was herself a schizophrenic and in receipt of psychiatric support. In October 1993 the senior support worker at the community support unit caring for her expressed concern at the effect on her health of the continuing subtle harassment from Tenant A. On 6 January 1995 the Senior Management Officer sent a memo to the city solicitor expressing concern at the fact that Tenant A was harassing two tenants who themselves had mental health problems. The condition of one of these tenants was said to be deteriorating. Tenant G was later assaulted by Tenant A, and in August 1995 gave notice to quit her tenancy, in order to move in with a friend 'for mutual support'.

The son of another elderly tenant (H) telephoned the housing department to report that the noise and threats from Tenant A were making his father ill. At least one other complainant was reported to be ill as a result of his behaviour, and one of the main victims of the harassment was herself emotionally very vulnerable following the murder of her daughter who was a prostitute. Moreover, two of the residents were involved in an altercation which was itself prompted by Tenant A's behaviour.

At the same time, fears were also expressed for Tenant A's own safety, both by his neighbours and also by housing officials. In December 1993 Tenant G telephoned to say that Tenant A appeared to be out of control, was neglecting himself, playing loud music and hurling abuse at nobody in particular. Social services were contacted out of concern for his well-being. Following the flooding at the new premises, fears were also expressed for Tenant A's safety since there was felt to be a serious risk of retaliation by some of his neighbours.

Quite apart from the risk of physical violence, neighbour disputes can drag on for years,[14] during which time they may often exact a heavy toll on the physical and emotional well-being of those involved, and also their families. This is particularly likely in cases where, for one reason or another, the formal legal remedies are inapplicable. In some neighbour nuisance cases, the tenant who is complained of may not be directly responsible for the anti-social behaviour, and may be at least as much a victim as the neighbours making the complaints, as in the next example.[15]

Case history 7

In January 1996 the caretaker of a block of flats owned by Council A reported that he had received a large number of complaints alleging banging, continuous shouting, abusive language and behaviour from one of the flats. Housing officials discovered that most of the disturbance was caused not by the tenant herself but her boyfriend, who had broken into the property, stole her keys and regularly assaulted her. Although the victim of repeated acts of serious domestic violence, she was afraid to proceed with a prosecution and seemed reluctant to leave him in spite of the violence and despite being offered alternative accommodation. Among the neighbours who were disturbed and distressed by the boyfriend's behaviour an elderly couple in the upstairs flat had been particularly badly affected, and had applied for a transfer as a result.

Cases illustrating the financial costs of neighbour disputes for those directly involved and also in relation to public funds

For the minority of disputants who seek to resolve their neighbour disputes by utilising conventional legal remedies there may also be severe financial consequences, and in very many cases such responses prove to be ineffective and inappropriate, or even counter-productive, as well as time-consuming. Evidence of the cost and limitations of conventional legal remedies was uncovered during the small-scale content analysis study of newspaper reports which we conducted as part of the current project.

Case history 8[16]

A dispute over a fast-growing *Cupressus leylandii* hedge began in 1979 with an exchange of solicitors' letters and ended up seventeen years later in the Court of Appeal, by which time the legal fees were estimated at £100,000. Although the court upheld a householder's right to trim his neighbour's boundary hedge, the victor complained that the dispute had cost him his life savings, as a result of which he and his wife had been obliged to forego holidays and other luxuries. And even though his neighbour was ordered to pay £44,000 towards the complainant's legal costs, he had responded by planting another row of trees. Since these were situated six feet behind the garden boundary they would be beyond the reach of the law.

Case history 9[17]

In 1995 a long-running feud between two neighbours culminated in a three day hearing in the House of Lords after a two-week hearing in the County Court and a three day hearing in the Court of Appeal had failed to resolve the 'important point of law involved'. The fourteen year dispute came to a head in 1989 when a housewife (Mrs. A) complained repeatedly to the police that her neighbour (Mr. B) had indecently exposed himself on the other side of her garden fence. Although Mr. B was arrested and charged, no evidence was offered and the case was dropped. The two neighbours then each took out private prosecutions for assault after

complaining unsuccessfully to the police, and this time Mrs. A succeeded in her action.

Mr. B then sued her in the County Court for malicious prosecution over the indecent exposure charge, and Mrs. A counter-claimed alleging malicious prosecution in respect of Mr. B's unsuccessful prosecution for assault. Both neighbours succeeded in their actions, the County Court awarding Mr. B £3,500 and his neighbour, Mrs. A, £550. Mrs. A succeeded in her appeal against the award in the Court of Appeal, but Mr. B then appealed to the House of Lords and was ultimately successful. Mrs. A was ordered to pay Mr. B's Court of Appeal costs, estimated at around £20,000, but since she was granted legal aid for the House of Lords hearing, the combined costs for this final phase of the battle (which are likely to have been in excess of £50,000) were met by the legal aid fund.

Case history 10[18]

In 1984 the miners' strike embittered relations between two neighbours, a village policeman and a miner, who had previously been good friends in the West Yorkshire pit village in which they lived. As relations deteriorated, the police officer put his house up for sale, but failed to find a buyer and went on long-term sick leave in 1991, suffering from depression. In 1995 an action was begun in Leeds County Court, involving numerous claims and counter-claims. Most of these were dismissed by the judge, who accused both parties of embroidering and distorting the truth. Each litigant was awarded £75 against the other, though the costs of the case, estimated at a five-figure sum, were met by the public purse since both parties were on legal aid.

Case history 11[19]

In May 1996, the Guardian newspaper reported on a complex series of disputes involving the residents of various flats situated in an elegant Edwardian house in the London suburb of Hampstead. In 1973, a series of relatively minor complaints over noise and damage to a bath-room ceiling resulting from overflowing bath water in an upstairs flat quickly degenerated into a protracted and increasingly bitter dispute.

The intensity of the hatred and ill-will that

has built up over the years is belied by the apparent triviality of many of the incidents that have been the subject of complaint – ranging from the position of the residents' milk bottles and building of a snow-man on the driveway to the dangling of some blocks of Lego over a balcony, the smell of meat sizzling on a barbecue, the use of security lights and the noise of feet tramping up and down the common stairs.

Attempts to resolve the dispute by conventional legal methods have resulted in a number of civil and criminal court hearings and have involved 'at least 25 separate firms of solicitors' over the years. The best endeavours of the political establishment have also proved unequal to the task, despite the interventions of two successive Attorney Generals[20] and two prominent Labour M.P.s (Paul Boateng and Glenda Jackson).

The conflict is estimated to have cost one of the disputants over £1 million comprising:

- cost of legal action already undertaken and paid for £250,000
- bankruptcy claims £363,484
- cost of bankruptcy fees £200,000
- legal aid to be repaid (estimated) £200,000
- Outstanding claim by another pair of residents £86,441
- Outstanding claim by a firm of London builders £76,363
- Total amount £1,176,288

This same resident, who was reported to have instituted ten sets of legal proceedings against her near neighbours since 1982 is now bankrupt, having lost her claim to legal aid, and faces forcible eviction from her home.

A second resident was charged with assaulting his neighbour after an incident in the hallway, but was acquitted by a jury. He complained that the 'obsessive litigation' associated with the conflict had cost him and his wife £150,000 in legal fees, though he was awarded £22,000 from his neighbour (who also owns the freehold of the property) for failing to keep the house in good repair, and she has since been ordered to pay costs and damages

totalling over £86,000 following an unsuccessful counter-claim .

Although the financial costs incurred as a result of the dispute have been astronomical, the human and emotional costs of the dispute appear to have been equally crippling. Thus, a third resident was reported to have said that she was unable to talk about the house as she was still recovering from an emotional break-down induced by the tension created by events that happened 20 years ago, while a fourth resident complained of having been driven out of the property as a result of 'malicious and vexatious hounding'.

As we have seen, few people who are involved in a dispute with their neighbours resort to legal remedies, and not all of these are awarded legal aid, so the total cost to the legal aid budget is almost certainly relatively small, even though the sums involved in some individual cases may seem very large. However, public expenditure is also incurred where neighbour disputes involve the intervention of agencies such as the police, or local authority officials from housing, environmental services or other departments such as social services or legal departments. The numbers involved here are very much greater, and in the next chapter we set out to illustrate and quantify some of the costs that are involved in respect of local authority housing, legal and administration and environmental health departments.

Notes

1 Guardian, 31 May 1995; 1 December 1995; 2 April 1996

2 Independent, 20 March 1993

3 Guardian, 28 February 1996

4 Times, 22 June 1996

5 The Independent, 18 December 1994. In a recent Parliamentary debate (on the second reading of the Noise Bill) Mr. Hawksley claimed that more than 20 people had died as a result of noise disputes with their neighbours since 1992, 16 February 1996, H.C. Deb. vol. 271. col 1255.

6 We are not suggesting that these cases would necessarily have been suitable for mediation. Indeed, it would be almost impossible to infer whether or not this was the case on the basis of the limited information reported in the media. The sole purpose of these case histories is to highlight how serious the consequences can be when neighbour disputes do get out of hand. We discuss in more detail the kinds of cases for which mediation might or might not be suitable in Chapter 10.

7 Guardian, 13 and 28 September 1995.

8 Times, 14 February 1996

9 Times, 20 March 1996

10 Times, 7 August 1996

11 During the course of the research we examined a large number of individual property files belonging to two separate local authority housing departments in the north of England. In many cases the files contained detailed evidence relating to various kinds of neighbour disputes, their effects on those involved, and the actions taken to resolve the problem. A number of these have been written up as case histories while compiling the present report.

12 Council A. Because of concerns over the issue of commercial confidentiality arising from the introduction of compulsory competitive tendering, we undertook not to disclose the identity of any of the departments that agreed to act as 'case studies'.

13 In the case history that follows, we only summarise the main events and complaints. Consequently, not all the complaining tenants are referred to; nevertheless we have retained the initials we used to refer to them in the original case notes.

14 While investigating the cost of dealing with neighbour disputes we came across one dispute which had been ongoing for upwards of ten years and was still unresolved.

15 Even though the recent change in the law brought about by the Housing Act 1996, which we referred to earlier, now makes it easier for social landlords to seek possession in such circumstances, it may still be difficult to persuade a court that it would be reasonable to evict a tenant who is herself the victim of the anti-social behaviour being complained of by others.

16 Times, 2 April 1996.

17 Guardian, 6 June 1995 and 14 July 1995.

18 Times, 4 June 1996

19 Guardian, 8 May 1996; reported by David Hencke and Edward Pilkington with additional reporting by James Wilson.

20 Sir Patrick Mayhew who was reported to have begun proceedings to debar one of the protagonists as a vexatious litigant and Sir Nicholas Lyell who dropped the matter.

Assessing the cost of neighbour disputes for social landlords

Identifying the range of costs incurred by social landlords

Of all the agencies that are affected by neighbour disputes, social landlords are in a unique position. As landlords, they are not only responsible for dealing with neighbour disputes in which their tenants may be involved but are themselves likely to be affected in a variety of ways by some of the consequences to which neighbour disputes can all too often give rise. It is important to take into account this dual role of social landlords – as 'intermediaries' and also as 'indirect victims' – when seeking to compare the costs of different ways of tackling the problem; and in identifying the scope for any savings that might be attainable by dealing with neighbour disputes more effectively.

In this chapter we begin by attempting to identify more precisely the full range of costs that are likely to be incurred by housing departments as a result of neighbour disputes. These are depicted in the form of a chart in Figure 6.1.

As 'intermediaries', the responsibility for dealing with neighbour disputes is likely to fall principally on housing officers working within the local authority's area housing offices, and their immediate and senior managers. The costs involved here are mainly the direct salary costs and associated overheads relating to the time spent dealing with neighbour disputes. These are depicted in the dark green boxes in Figure 6.1 and are relatively easy to determine provided the amount of time spent on neighbour disputes can be reliably ascertained. These costs also provide the most appropriate basis[1] on which to compare informal interventions by housing departments with alternative methods of dealing with neighbour disputes such as mediation.

Some other costs are also incurred by social landlords as a direct result of their intervention as intermediaries and these are shown in the pale green boxes in Figure 6.1. For example, one response to a neighbour dispute might be to rehouse one of the parties. We consider the extent to which these costs can be quantified later in this chapter, and will return to this issue again in Chapter 9.

In other cases, the response might involve the threat or use of legal action against one of the parties. We examine the cost implications that are associated with this course of action in Chapter 7.

However, these are by no means the only costs that are likely to be incurred by social landlords as a result of neighbour disputes, particularly where these prove difficult to resolve.

As landlords, local authority housing departments and Housing Associations have a direct stake in the successful resolution of neighbour disputes, whatever approach is used, since the consequences of failure can be costly. These other consequential costs are also set out in Figure 6.1 although, as we shall see, the extent to which they can be accurately quantified is highly variable.

In the sections that follow, we first explain how we attempted to quantify the direct salary costs[2] involved in dealing with neighbour disputes, and how this approach can be applied to a sample of individual case histories in order to ascertain the cost of informal intervention in relation to specific neighbour disputes.

Then we go on to consider the other 'consequential' costs to which neighbour disputes might also give rise, and the extent to which they can also be accurately quantified. Although it is not appropriate (nor indeed is it always possible) to incorporate all of these consequential costs for the purpose of comparing mediation with informal intervention by social landlords, they do nevertheless represent potential savings from which the local authority might be expected to benefit if a more effective method could be found for dealing with neighbour disputes.[3]

Figure 6.1: Costs of neighbour disputes to local authority housing departments.

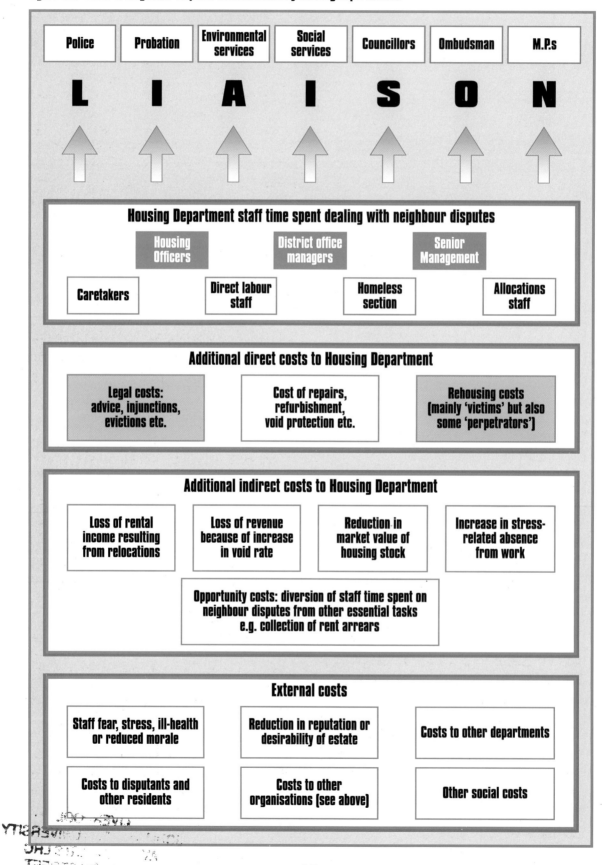

Ascertaining the cost of informal intervention by social landlords

Little information is publicly available regarding the cost to local authorities of dealing with neighbour disputes. As part of our general survey of social landlords, we asked respondents to estimate the proportion of housing officers' time that is devoted to responding directly to neighbour nuisance complaints, or liaising with colleagues or other council departments or agencies about the action that should be taken.

The results are set out in Table 6.1, and show that neighbour disputes are thought to take up almost a fifth of housing officer's time, which is broadly in line with other reported estimates (Aldbourne Associates, 1993: 3). There is relatively little variation between council types, and only the solitary response from a housing association representative was seriously out of line with the rest.

These global estimates are relatively imprecise, however, and we therefore sought more detailed information relating to the time actually spend dealing with neighbour disputes in respect of our three local authority case study areas, based, where possible, on time monitoring exercises. These invariably show a much lower figure.

In Council B, for example, key performance indicators relating to the five sets of housing teams for 1995/6 showed that a total of 2,837 staff hours were spent on neighbour dispute cases out of a total of 295,048 hours available for the calendar year as a whole. This suggests that just over one per cent of total staff time available was devoted to neighbour disputes, though it should be noted that the figure includes all grades of staff and represents the average

for the council as a whole. The amount of time spent by individual housing officers working in some of the more difficult estates is likely to be considerably more than this.

In Council A, the results of a limited time monitoring exercise carried out in two housing areas in June/July 1994 suggested that while the total amount of staff time devoted to neighbour disputes averaged 1.5%, the average for management and senior management officers was 8.5%, and the average for area managers and assistant area managers was 6.8% of their total time.

In Council C it is estimated that 22 estate officers and 27 assistant estate officers devote 12.5% of their time on average to neighbour disputes. In addition, two officers with specific responsibilities for recording cases, monitoring noise and nuisance, preparing witness statements and initiating legal proceedings are reported to spend 95% of their time dealing with neighbour disputes. Neighbour disputes are also said to account for 5% of the time of 8 senior management officers and for 2% of the time of the general manager and assistant chief housing officer.

When it comes to quantifying the costs involved, it is a relatively straightforward matter[4] to calculate the salary costs and associated overheads. However, there is a major problem as we have seen, concerning the availability, accessibility and reliability of information relating to the amount of time spent specifically on neighbour dispute cases.

Few councils monitor this kind of data centrally, and local area offices vary considerably in their record-keeping practices. Moreover, few individual offices have undertaken time-monitoring exercises, and those that are conducted tend to be only of short duration. In the absence of such time-monitoring data, the only way of reliably ascertaining the amount of time spent on neighbour disputes is to comb through the relevant housing files and ascertain the actions taken and the grades of housing officers involved. Those who were involved in the case can then be asked to estimate how long they spent on each task.

Because of the difficulties we encountered collecting and collating sufficiently detailed information relating to individual neighbour disputes, and also gaining access to the relevant financial data required, we decided to concentrate in this part of

Table 6.1: Estimates of the proportion of Housing Officers' time devoted to dealing with neighbour disputes, by type of department.

Type of department	Estimated proportion (%)	No. of Departments on which based
City	20.3	6
District/Borough	18.3	3
Metropolitan	17.5	2
London Borough	13.8	2
Housing assoc.	5.0	1
Overall	17.5	14

Source of data: Mediation research project national survey of Housing departments

43

LIVERPOOL JOHN MOORES UNIVERSITY AVRIL ROBARTS LRC TITHEBARN STREET LIVERPOOL L2 2ER TEL. 0151 231 4022

the study on a single local authority – Council A – which is a large urban council in the north of England. Council A resembles other large urban authorities in devolving the administration of its housing services to a number of local area offices.

One of these offices, serving area 'a', appeared to keep particularly detailed records in relation to neighbour disputes, but in other respects seemed to be reasonably representative of many urban local authority housing districts both within Council A and indeed around the country. Area 'a' was therefore selected for a detailed case study, the aim of which was to provide an overview of the direct costs incurred in respect of neighbour disputes within a single housing area as a result of informal interventions by housing officers over a twelve month period.[5] All actions taken in response to neighbour nuisance complaints during this period (whether in respect of new or existing cases) were collated, and the times recorded.[6]

The exercise thus provided a 'snap-shot' view of the time devoted to nuisance complaints by housing service staff during a prescribed period, rather than a 'cradle-to-grave' costing from beginning to end of each neighbour dispute case, of the kind we undertook in respect of the community mediation services,[7] and also in relation to the case histories we examined. Nevertheless, it was the closest approximation we were able to devise for any of the housing departments we had canvassed as part of our general survey.

We examined the relevant property files themselves[8] in order to ascertain what action had been taken during the monitoring period, how long it took, and whether there had been any further action or evidence of a further dispute between the ending of the monitoring exercise in December 1994 and June 1996, when the research was carried out. We also recorded any relevant information on the files relating to outcome (including whether one or more of the parties appeared to have moved as a result of the dispute).

By apportioning each action taken to the relevant grade of staff, and applying the appropriate on-costs we were able to ascertain the full direct costs incurred by staff working within the housing area in respect of those disputes on which action was taken during the relevant monitoring period. However, for disputes that started before or continued beyond the

monitoring period, the figures we recorded would only represent part of the total cost involved, and to that extent the figures are not directly comparable with those we calculated for community mediation services.

Case study 1 – urban housing area case study

Case study 1 relates to a housing area situated in a large urban local authority – Council A – in the north of England. The tenure profile for housing area 'a' comprises 49.6% Local Authority dwellings, 2.9% Housing Association dwellings, 3.7% privately rented dwellings and 43.8% owner occupied dwellings. The Local Authority housing consists of 5022 houses, 549 purpose built flats, 115 converted flats and 1 bedsit.

The area has an unemployment rate of 15%. Forty three percent of households do not have a wage earner and 9% of households with children have no wage earner. In terms of ethnic composition the area is predominantly white (94.5%).

The Housing Office will only investigate a case if the tenant puts the complaint in writing or goes to the Area Office to make a statement. It is felt that this policy gives the tenants the opportunity to resolve the problem themselves and also to consider whether they really want the housing department's involvement. The area housing office urges tenants to resolve their own problems by speaking to their neighbour and will only become involved where the tenant cannot or will not do this, or where tenants' own attempts at a resolution have failed.

The office receives a large number of enquiries which go no further. These were not recorded on the data file on which the costings were based. In addition, there may have been actions which have not been recorded. The data file thus gives a conservative estimate of the actions taken in a case. Likewise, the economic costings will almost certainly not capture the total costs involved in dealing with neighbour disputes even though we have tried to ensure that they are as complete as possible. In particular, they only show the direct salary costs involved, though we do discuss the other direct and indirect costs and the extent to which it is possible to quantify these later in the chapter.

One dispute in area 'a' had continued for ten

years, though the Senior Management Officer considered this to be unusual. Four or five other cases had been ongoing for a period of more than a year. The Area Manager felt that out of around 6,000 tenants there were 50 to 100 who caused problems for other tenants.

Over the 1994 calendar year as a whole, action was taken in respect of 117 neighbour disputes. Visits were made to at least one of the parties in 77% of cases[9], and warning letters were sent to one of the parties in 19% of the cases.[10] The total time spent on neighbour disputes by area 'a' officers of all grades was estimated at 203 hours, which was equivalent to only 0.6% of the total housing officer time available (excluding other staff such as caretakers and benefits team). In financial terms, we calculate that the total full cost[11] of dealing with neighbour disputes in area 'a' was £5,764.10 which is equivalent to 1.2% of the total budget (again excluding the cost of other staff such as caretakers).

As for the 'unit cost' per case dealt with, our summary findings relating to this part of the project are set out in Table 6.2. These show that, on average, housing officers spent a total of 1.74 hours on each neighbour dispute in which they were asked to intervene during the period covered by the survey, which means that the full direct cost to the housing department averaged £49.24 per case.

These figures should be treated with caution, however, since they are likely to seriously underestimate the total resource costs incurred for each case. In the first place, as we have seen, several of the disputes are likely to have 'straddled' the monitoring period at either side, meaning that the time spent on actions taken outside this period will not have been captured by the annual cost figures. It thus seems probable that in a number of cases additional costs would have been incurred in respect of actions taken outside the monitoring period.

Secondly, the times recorded for specific actions taken in relation to a dispute are likely to provide a conservative estimate of the total time devoted to a case. For example, there may well have been other actions (such as telephone calls, informal conversations with the parties or with colleagues concerning the case) which were not recorded, and for which no times are therefore available.

Thirdly, the area concerned did not appear to have undertaken any expensive formal action against tenants during the monitoring period, which would almost certainly have increased the average costs incurred. It is known that,[12] in the twelve months prior to September 1995 there had been no evictions; 12 NSPs (Notices of Intent to Seek Possession) had been served for nuisance but no tenants had been taken to court. No injunctions had been applied for. Professional witnesses had been used on three occasions to investigate a total of 12 tenancies.[13]

Fourthly, the times recorded for even the most labour-intensive cases dealt with by area 'a' within the survey period seemed considerably shorter than the amount of time spent over a twelve month period on some of the case histories we examined, which were drawn from other housing areas within Council A (see below).

This raises the possibility that, compared with these other housing areas, area 'a' might have been atypical in terms of either the number or type of neighbour nuisance complaints it received, or the way these were dealt with; alternatively it might have been experiencing an unusually quiescent period.

The first of these possibilities seems unlikely. Area 'a' has a high proportion of local authority housing (50%), some of which comprises estates that are known to be difficult to manage. Moreover, in two previous time monitoring exercises conducted over shorter periods[14] and involving a number of housing areas within Council A, area 'a' was generally at or near the top of the league in terms of the average times spent on neighbour nuisance complaints.

If the results of these earlier exercises are 'extrapolated' over a whole year, the total number of hours devoted to neighbour nuisance cases

Table 6.2: Neighbour dispute costs incurred by Council A housing area 'a' in respect of a twelve month period, based on actual case records.

Caseload	117
Av. hrs per case	1.74
Full costs per case	£49.27
'Imputed cost'	£245.18

within area 'a' comes to 144 hours and 370 hours respectively. Thus, we can probably also discount the possibility that the period under review was exceptionally quiescent.

This leaves the possibility that area 'a' might differ from some other housing areas in terms of the way neighbour disputes are dealt with. There is some support for this hypothesis in the form of another time monitoring exercise which was conducted by two other housing areas within Council A over short (4 week) periods in June and July 1994.

Unlike the two earlier time monitoring exercises (mentioned above) this one did seek to apportion the proportion of time spent on neighbour nuisance monitoring to the different grades of staff, as we did in our own study. This suggested that a much higher proportion of total staff time in these areas was devoted to neighbour nuisance complaints across all grades of staff than we had found to be the case in respect of area 'a'.[15]

One explanation for the discrepancy might be that staff in these other two areas adopted a much more 'intensive' approach when dealing with neighbour disputes, compared with staff in area 'a'. It would be difficult to discount this possibility without further close investigation of possible differences in approach and management style (or differences in recording practice).

In order to see what difference it would make to our findings if staff involvement were as intensive as these other figures suggest, we averaged the two sets of figures derived from these earlier studies and applied them to our own calculations to give the 'imputed' figure shown in Table 6.2 above. As can be seen, the effect is quite dramatic, since the average cost per case calculated on the basis of these figures is five times greater, at £245.18.

Another explanation for the discrepancy, which also seems plausible, is that the level of staff input, and thus the resource cost to the departments, is influenced not so much by the number of neighbour nuisance complaints as their level of intractability. It seems quite probable that a small number of difficult-to-handle neighbour disputes (of the kind we examine in the next section) could exert a disproportionate effect on a housing department area's budget in relation to their numbers. As

we have suggested, it seems that area 'a' might have had fewer of these difficult-to-handle disputes than other Council A housing areas during the period in question. Thus, the most expensive neighbour dispute case that was dealt with by staff in area 'a' during the relevant period was £276.16 which, as we shall see, is very much less than the annual expenditure incurred for several of the case histories we examined, both in Council A and B.[16]

However, a fifth and much more substantial reason for treating the figures in Table 6.2 with caution is that, as we have explained, they only relate to the direct salary and associated costs that are incurred by housing area staff. As Figure 6.1 makes clear, these represent only a part (and in some neighbour dispute cases only a very small part) of the total resource cost to the housing department and the council as a whole that might properly be attributable to neighbour disputes, even in respect of the former's role as intermediary. We examine the extent to which it is possible to quantify the additional costs we have identified later in the chapter.

Assessing the cost of informal interventions in specific cases

In the next section, we narrow the focus in an attempt to illustrate the costs of informal interventions by local authority housing departments in some of the individual neighbour dispute cases they are called upon to deal with, especially some of the more intractable ones. The case histories that follow all originated within Council A. We selected four area offices (approximately one in four) within the Council's Housing Department, each of which had a different mix of housing types and neighbour dispute problems. The disputes outlined in the case histories are 'difficult' but by no means atypical.

For every dispute we have examined in this way we set out to identify as completely as we could from the written records every action taken by housing officers in relation to the dispute, and then asked the officials concerned to estimate the relevant times involved. We used this information to calculate as accurately as possible[17] the full resource costs incurred in dealing with these cases – but only in relation to the housing department itself.[18] The aim here was to illustrate the financial costs that can be, and frequently are, involved when dealing with cases which prove difficult to resolve.

We are not suggesting that some or all of the costs incurred in these cases could have been avoided had mediation been used instead. Indeed, in some of them it would appear most unlikely that mediation could have been deployed successfully. Nevertheless, in attempting to assess the scope for mediation to deal with neighbour disputes more cheaply or more effectively than existing procedures, it is also important to be able to identify the kinds of cases for which it would not be suitable. We return to the issue comparative costs and the scope for savings in Chapter 9, and we discuss the kind of cases for which mediation might be appropriate in Chapter 10.

The first three case histories were dealt with by the local area housing office in area 'b', and we begin by briefly describing its tenure profile and main demographic characteristics.

Area 'b' profile

The tenure profile for area 'b' comprises 72.1% Local Authority dwellings, 3.2% Housing Association dwellings, 2.3% privately rented dwellings and 22.4% owner occupied dwellings. The local authority housing consists of 3,555 houses, 1,051 purpose built flats and 2 converted flats.

The area has an unemployment rate of 24%. Fifty nine percent of households do not have a wage earner and 12% of households with children have no wage earner. As in area 'a', the ethnic composition in area 'b' is predominantly white (98.5).

According to the Housing Department Area Manager, this is a particularly stressed part of the City with a high level of poverty and criminality. Many of the neighbour disputes result from a clash of lifestyles brought about by inappropriate Housing allocation. Accommodation which was originally designated for the elderly is frequently allocated to younger people because it is available and there are no older people on the list to fill it. Problems caused by a clash of lifestyles are often aggravated by illegal activities such as drug abuse and burglary. Many of the disputes dealt with in the area do involve criminal activity and violence. Case history 12, below, is a good illustration of this type of dispute. As the landlord, the Housing department is often asked to intervene in issues which are really police matters. It is often a case of advising the tenants to contact the police.

Many of the complaints are about the teenage sons and daughters of tenants, or have to do with problems caused by former partners. Many young women who are allocated properties are exploited by boyfriends or former boyfriends and their associates who may take advantage of the tenancy for illegal or illicit activity such as drug abuse or, in the case of flats, using their access to communal areas to facilitate burglary of the other flats.

The Area Housing Office will always investigate formal complaints, at least to some extent, even if there appears to be nothing on the surface. What is really happening may not always be apparent to begin with, as seems possibly to have been the case with case history 13 (see page 49, below). Noise cases tend to be referred to Environmental Health. The local area manager feels that some of the cases may be amenable to mediation.[19] However, mediation may not be a suitable solution for cases involving illegal activity. The Housing Office will not consider using mediation in cases of racial harassment. In such cases, they will attempt to identify those responsible and take them to court. Case history 14 (see page 50) illustrates a fairly typical neighbour dispute in which mediation was felt by housing services and one of the parties to be appropriate, and indeed appears to have been attempted at one stage, though ultimately this approach was rejected by the party initiating the complaints.

Case history 12[20]

In this dispute, initial complaints relating to noise, vandalism, graffiti and harassment were made by a tenant in a block of flats. The disturbances were alleged to have been caused by visitors to one of the flats in the block, but proof of this was lacking, particularly in relation to some of the earlier incidents. Subsequently, there were complaints that the same tenant was keeping a dog and two cats, allowed the dog to defecate in the communal entrance and threw rubbish and faeces out of the windows. On several occasions the original complainant complained on behalf of one or more fellow residents, and later there were complaints from a number of the residents acting together, as well as from a further tenant acting individually.

The tenant against whom the complaints were directed was the sole tenant of the flat, but previously she had shared a joint tenancy with her boyfriend who quit his part of the tenancy following these complaints. The tenant and the boyfriend were initially housed in the flat because the boyfriend's previous flat had been burnt out. He had also been attacked and had received death threats.

The situation was exacerbated because the flats were initially intended for older people and most of the other residents were elderly. Housing of young single people and young couples in such premises is considered undesirable by the Housing Department but they often have no choice when these premises become empty and there are no elderly people with priority on the waiting list.

A complete chronology of the dispute, summarising all actions recorded in the relevant housing file together with the time taken to complete them, and also the cumulative costs to the Housing department is set out in Appendix 3. Briefly, the dispute lasted between 6 June 1995 and the date when the case history was concluded on 11 April 1996. During this time at least 17 separate sets of complaints (including sets of diary sheets) were logged by the housing area office.

Housing officers visited or interviewed complainants on at least five separate occasions, and visited or interviewed the tenant whose behaviour was being complained of on three separate occasions. The initial response to the complaints was to persuade the tenant's partner to quit his part of the tenancy, and to insist on the signing of new tenancy agreement that specifically forbade the keeping of dogs and cats. When these proved ineffective, complainants were issued with diary sheets and warnings were issued to the tenant regarding the noise and her failure to get rid of the dog.

However, Housing Department officials believed that the tenant was as much a victim as the other residents in the flats. It was thought that many of the problems resulted from use of the flat for drug taking and substance abuse by acquaintances of the tenant or her boyfriend. They included repeated damage to the communal door and lock, damage to the flat itself, since the door was repeatedly forced and several windows were smashed. It was thought probable that the tenant was being forced to allow these activities and,

towards the end of the log of events, the tenant may not even have been present when incidents took place.

One of the later diary sheets reported that 'a riot' had broken out on the evening of 10 April 1996, as a result of which 'a lot of windows were broken'. The police were called, and also an ambulance, which took the tenant to hospital for breathing difficulties following an assault.

Eventually it was decided to seek possession of the flat, and assistance was sought from the Administration and Legal Department. Before notice was served, however, and after consultation with the tenant's mother, the tenant was sent a letter guaranteeing rehousing in similar accommodation, with a warning that failure to comply with these arrangements would leave the Department with no option but to begin repossession proceedings.

The situation was finally resolved, at least as far as these premises were concerned, when the tenant was taken into hospital following the assault on 10 April. With the assistance of the tenant's mother she was persuaded to leave the flat with a guarantee of rehousing. The intention was to move her closer to her mother and away from the acquaintances who were abusing the flat. It was acknowledged, however, that these acquaintances would probably find her again.

Over the ten months that had elapsed between the initial complaints and the completion of the case history, the dispute had consumed an estimated 14.3 hours of housing officers' time, at an estimated direct cost of £209.67. This does not include the substantial sums that appear to have been spent by the council on repeated repairs to the property and in cleaning up graffiti and rubbish, nor the cost to other agencies such as the Administration and Legal department, the police and health services.

This was a case in which there appeared to be very limited scope for mediation[21] since the tenant appeared to be powerless to control the behaviour of her partner and other visitors to the flat.

Case history 13

This dispute involved an elderly couple who complained of deliberate noise, abuse and harassment from their neighbours. The elderly couple had been resident at the house for around fifty years. The neighbours, a family consisting of two parents and three children had lived at the address for approximately four years. The complaint was mainly brought to the Housing Department via the elderly couple's son who did not live with his parents, though the latter are referred to as the complainants.

The first entry on the relevant property file was dated 6 January 1994. Following an incident on 16 April to which the police were called, seven taxis arrived at the complainants' house during the course of the night, necessitating further police involvement. The son then complained to the area housing office by telephone and letter. The initial response by the housing officer was to inform the local community police officer who agreed to visit the elderly couple and report back. Visits were made by housing officials to both parties to the dispute, but the alleged perpetrators denied there was a problem, unless of the complainant's making. For their part, the elderly couple indicated that they no longer wished for any further action to be taken.

Further complaints were made, but most of these were instigated by the elderly couple's son. He repeatedly alleged that his parents were intimidated by and lived in fear of their neighbours, though it is not clear what part this played in their seeming reluctance to take the matter further, or even to complete a diary of events in relation to the noise complaints, as had been suggested.

At this stage it is clear that the area housing office took the view that not all the complaints were well-founded and, since the couple had previously complained about neighbours living on the other side who were also relatively new tenants with children, it was concluded that the complainants just did not wish to have young families as neighbours.

From around September 1995 – around 20 months into the dispute – the dispute appeared to be at least as much to do with the way the complaints had been handled by the council's

housing officers as with the original grievances, and only one fresh incident was reported after this.

In response to a letter from the complainant's MP, the Senior Management Officer wrote explaining that while both parties clearly had problems with one another, neither was in breach of their tenancy agreement and, although the police had been called on several occasions by both neighbours, no charges had been brought. Consequently, no action would be taken for the time being. The letter also stated that, while the complainants' neighbours had indicated that they would be prepared to attend a mediation service, it was believed that the complainants would be unwilling to do so.

It was not clear from the file whether the possibility of mediation had by this stage been raised with either party, and this was one of a number of points on which the complainants' son took issue in subsequent correspondence with both the council and the MP. The first recorded mention of mediation being actively encouraged was in a letter sent to the complainants' son by the Senior Management Officer on 20 October 1995, which also enclosed a leaflet advertising the local community mediation service.

In January 1996 the complainants' son wrote to the Director of Housing complaining about his department's handling of his parents' problems with their neighbours. Until this point the area office was still refusing to take the matter any further in view of the complainants' unwillingness to proceed with the complaint. However, in March 1996 the Area Manager offered to meet the complainants' son, and during the interview which followed, the possibility of using professional witnesses was discussed.

Subsequent investigations by the Area Manager revealed that the complainants' neighbours could actually be involved in illegal activity, and that the noise late at night might be a result of this. At the time the case history was concluded the matter was being investigated by the police.

Over its 26-month life-span the dispute had by this stage occupied an estimated 17.75 hours of housing officer time, involving personnel at virtually every level in the department. The estimated direct costs to the Housing Department are estimated at £333.23. Despite the active involvement of all these officials, the police and the MP concerned, the dispute had still not been resolved by the time the case history was written up.

The scope for mediation in this particular case is unclear. The possibility does not appear to have been mentioned until nineteen months into the dispute, by which time it was clearly too late, since attitudes had already become entrenched. Had it been attempted earlier, the prospects might have been much better. At the very least it might have provided a non-threatening environment in which the concerns of the elderly tenants themselves could have been raised and addressed.

Case history 14

There was some evidence that an attempt at mediation was made in the next case, but again this did not take place until twelve months after the original complaint, by which time the complainants had evidently been issued with diary sheets which they appeared to be filling in prior to, and after, the attempted mediation. The optimum timing for attempts at mediation and the circumstances in which it is most likely to succeed are issues we return to in Chapter 10. Meanwhile, it is worth remembering that where mediation is unsuccessful, as in this case, additional costs will also be incurred. However, it is also worth noting that conventional attempts to resolve the matter appear to have been no more successful in this case than mediation was.

The complainant in this dispute was not the actual tenant of the local authority but the nephew of the tenant, though they both resided at the house together with another adult relative. The complainant's family had been resident at the house since the mid 1930s. The complaints were directed against a family who lived at an adjoining house. This family consisted of two parents and four children aged between 12 and 19. They had been resident at the house since mid 1990.

The complainant first contacted the housing office in August 1992 to enquire about complaints procedures, but the initial complaint alleging excessive noise and rubbish being thrown over the garden and general area was made in February 1993. The housing department's initial response was to write to the complainant's neighbours

(following an unsuccessful attempt to visit them), drawing their attention to the terms of the tenancy agreement.

Although the problem appeared to have subsided for a while, further complaints mainly relating to DIY noise were made in early 1994, and in February the alleged perpetrators reported that they had attended the local mediation service, with whom the complainant had also been in contact. They stated that they had agreed to abide by an undertaking to inform their neighbours whenever they were intending to do any DIY work.

However, diaries recording incidents of excessive noise were received by the housing office relating to several periods between November 1993 and June 1994. In August 1994, the housing office received a letter complaining about the way the case had been dealt with and pressing for stronger action. These complaints were repeated during a visit by housing officers, during which the complainant threatened to retaliate against his neighbours. He was advised about his own conduct and also regarding the records to keep in the future, and further complaints were made over the next few weeks.

In October 1994 the family about whom the complaints had been received were interviewed and gave their side of the story. They outlined the problems they had experienced with the complainant's behaviour, which allegedly included attempts at provocation.

At this point, Environmental Health officers were brought in to investigate the complaints. Their finding that there were insufficient grounds for legal action confirmed the view of housing officers that there had been no breach of tenancy conditions, and that the complainant might indeed have been harassing his neighbour.

The complainant then began pressing for stronger action to be taken, and obtained the support of his MP and also a local councillor. A further complaint over the handling of the case was made at a meeting of the local community forum in February 1995. Housing officers undertook further investigations of the complaints in early 1995, following which the Area Manager wrote, explaining that there was insufficient evidence to support action either under the relevant noise nuisance legislation or in pursuit of an order for possession.

The letter concluded by strongly recommending mediation as the most appropriate course of action. By this stage the complainant had referred the matter to the Local Government Ombudsman, but in August 1995 he wrote advising that he had investigated the case and considered that the Council had thoroughly investigated the original complaints, and had taken all actions that were justified.

Since the investigation by the Local Government Ombudsman, the complainant sought appointments with the Area Housing Manager on a number of occasions, but none of these had been kept by the tenant. The complainant's neighbours indicated that they would still be happy to have another attempt at mediation, but the complainant refused to participate.

Over the three years since the complainant's original enquiry this dispute had consumed approximately 28.58 hours of housing officers' time at an estimated total cost of £565.86. The total elapsed time was 3.07 years, and the annualised case costs over this period were £184.08 per year.

The next five case histories relate to neighbour disputes that arose within the local area housing office serving Council A's area 'c'. Once again, we begin by briefly describing its tenure profile and main demographic characteristics.

Area 'c' profile

Area 'c' is centred on the city centre, which means that its geographical boundaries do not coincide with those for other services within Council A such as Environmental Health. Within the Environmental Health department areas spread out from a point in the city centre, which means that this particular housing area cuts across a number of environmental service boundaries. This has obvious repercussions in terms of the number of Environmental Health Officers with whom officers responsible for housing area 'c' have to liaise.

Area 'c' is also quite different from area 'b' in terms of its tenure profile. Here, the proportion of local authority dwellings is 15.4%, which compares with 61.2% owner occupied dwellings, 17.9% privately rented dwellings and 5.5% housing association dwellings. The local authority housing consists of 1,002 houses, 2,054 purpose built flats, 43 converted flats and 1 bedsit.

The local authority housing in this area is somewhat more scattered than in other areas of the City, and is more interspersed with private rented accommodation and dwellings with owner occupiers. The housing office will normally only act if both parties involved in a dispute are Council tenants.[22] There are more Tenant Associations in area 'c' than in other areas within Council A. Tenants' Associations were considered by the Senior Management Officer for the area to be instrumental in reporting many neighbour nuisance cases.

Possibly because of its proximity to the city centre, this Housing Area has a considerable number of tenants with mental health problems.[23] Seemingly, when a person suffering from psychiatric problems is released from hospital or discharged under the 'care in the community' initiative, Council A's social services department is supposed to liaise with the 'Care in the Community' team which operates within the Housing Department, and together they are supposed to work out an appropriate accommodation/support package for the person concerned.

However, according to the Area Manager for area 'c', this procedure is frequently not followed, and the person concerned is simply advised to present him- or herself to the homeless section. In any event, the Care in the Community team comprises only one officer, whose responsibilities cover the whole of the city. This can often result in unsuitable housing allocations which may increase the likelihood of friction or even more serious neighbour disputes (as we saw in case histories 5 and 6).

Finally, in terms of its social and ethnic profiles, the area has an unemployment rate of 14.3%. Forty per cent of households do not have a wage earner, and 5% of households with children have no wage earner. As in the other two areas we have looked at within Council A, the ethnic composition in area 'c' is predominantly white (89%).

The first case history involves a relatively straightforward, if protracted, neighbour nuisance dispute that appears on the face of it to be eminently suitable for mediation but for the fact that both parties refuse to give it a try when it is eventually suggested, after almost ten years of hostilities. The other cases are somewhat less straightforward, though all involve complaints alleging neighbour nuisance.

Case history 15

This dispute has been ongoing for a number of years. Tenant A has lived at the property since it was first built in November 1978. He now resides there with his wife and – until recently – their children, though the latter are believed to have moved out. Tenants B are approximately twenty years younger than their neighbours and have rented their house, where they live with their children, since April 1985. The dispute appears to have started soon after Tenants B moved in.

In September 1985 Tenant A complained of noise and dog fouling. He was advised to contact Environmental Health. In July 1987 Tenant A complained about the state of B's garden. Tenant B was sent a warning letter. Several other complaints followed between autumn 1987 and spring 1988, to which housing officers responded by attempting to visit B and (since these were mainly unsuccessful) by writing to them. Complaints then became more sporadic until June 1992 when Tenant A enquired about rehousing.

In response to a further complaint about noise in November 1992, a housing officer interviewed tenant B, who said he would try to keep down the noise made by his children. Since then there have been further complaints, mainly brought by A, who has accused his neighbours of assault, abuse, damage and misbehaviour by B's children; though B has also accused A of assault. In March 1995 both parties were bound over.

Complaints about B's behaviour continued through 1995, coupled with calls for stronger action (preferably eviction) by the council, and requests to be rehoused. Both parties brought charges against one another in October/November 1995, and around this time the police suggested giving mediation a try. A similar pattern prevailed over the following months, during which time B also made accusations against A. The housing office responded by writing to remind A of his tenancy obligations, and by emphasising its neutrality in the dispute.

A letter from the Area Manager to Tenant A in March 1996 summed up the Housing Department's view (and evident sense of frustration) by pointing out that the parties just don't get on and warning that if any action was taken it would be against both tenants for causing a general nuisance,

which could result in them both losing their tenancies. The letter also proposed mediation as an option, though this may have been borne of desperation rather than optimism after a dispute lasting more than ten years.

A subsequent complaint by another of B's neighbours who were owner-occupiers was rejected on the grounds that the Council could not act on their behalf since they were not their landlords.

At the time the case was written up the dispute was still ongoing. Tenant A was reluctant to move unless he could move to a property of a similar type, and such properties were not available for rehousing in such circumstances. Tenants B were unable to move because of rent arrears. The level of nuisance was not considered sufficiently serious for the Council to seek possession.

In the view of the Management Officer responsible for the case, both families were capable of being good neighbours but not to one another. He characterised the dispute as a personality clash and a lifestyle clash. Both neighbours have refused mediation though, as we have noted, by the time this possibility was first mooted, the dispute had been in existence for ten years.

Over this period it is estimated that the total amount of housing officers' time expended on the case was 22.3 hours, involving an estimated direct cost of £488.91 at current prices.[24]

Case history 16

This case is a good illustration of the kind of the problems associated with 'crime-related' neighbour disputes, of the kind described by the Area Manager responsible for area 'b'[25] and would appear to offer little scope for mediation. In April 1996 a report was received from the caretaker of a block of flats which contained allegations of theft of cars, arson and burglary, naming X, who was a tenant in the same block of flats.[26]

Tenant X was interviewed at the area office but denied all the allegations. X was warned that if he or visitors to his home were found to be responsible he would be evicted. A few days later an anonymous letter was received about X, and further allegations were made by the caretaker alleging that he had committed further acts of vandalism and arson of another car (described as the fourth). The housing officer informed the caretaker that such allegations were a matter for the police, and advised tenants to report them to the police. She also advised that in the absence of absolute proof and witnesses they would not be able to take action against the tenant.

Subsequently, the housing officer was in touch with both police and the tenant's probation officer requesting their intervention. The visit by the probation officer elicited further denials by tenant X, but concerns were raised over the fact that at the time of the visit there were three boys in the flat aged between 10 and 15, all of whom admitted to staying overnight on occasion. These concerns were relayed by the housing officer to Council A's social services department.

Further complaints about the behaviour of the tenant were made by an upstairs neighbour later that same month. A few days later, a housing officer took a statement from the caretaker of the flat and was in contact with a representative from the Tenants' Association in an attempt to obtain names and addresses of witnesses who might be willing to give statements about the incidents. However, those who might have assisted were said to be afraid to co-operate following threats.

Shortly afterwards tenant X himself phoned the area office to complain that a police officer had been to see him at the housing officer's request. Apparently X had denied being the person the police wished to question, despite being asked for both by the name he currently used and one that he had used in the past. X complained of being wrongly accused and harassed and was advised to make a formal complaint.

Since the allegations first came to light the council have used a professional witness, but have still been unable to gather any definite evidence about who is responsible for the incidents. The case was still ongoing at the time of writing, by which time it was estimated to have taken up at least ten full days of housing officers' time, despite its brief duration. The direct cost of this involvement is estimated at £911.42.[27]

Case history 17

The next neighbour nuisance case has principally come about as a result of drug abuse. The tenant who is the subject of the complaint is taking methadone in order to come off heroin. However, the main cause of the nuisance is not so much the tenant himself as the behaviour of his associates. Indeed, the tenant may possibly be as much of a victim as his neighbours, since he has himself been assaulted by them, and has had property stolen by them.[28]

On 16 January 1996 two housing officers visited the complainant, and also the tenant who was the subject of the complaint. The complainant stated that for some time she had been picking up needles from the communal area, and that her husband had been trying to bury these in his allotment(!). She also complained that there was a lot of noise at night when groups of the tenant's 'friends' came round to take drugs, which is when they left their needles. On one occasion the tenant had asked if he could use his next door neighbour's balcony in order to gain access to his property by kicking out the 'kick pad'. The housing officers advised the complainant to complete a diary of events, after which they would visit again.

In the event, the officers did not get to see the tenant who was the subject of complaint. Although he was in, he was 'unable' to unlock the door. The housing officers spoke to him through the locked door, advising him of the complaints and the finding of a needle. The tenant denied that this was possible, and agreed to come to the housing office the next day. He was advised that the council could serve a notice seeking possession for nuisance.

For several weeks after this visit things went quiet, but on 25 March 1996 the caretaker reported that one of the visitors to the tenant's flat had broken a large number of windows causing 'thousands of pounds worth of damage', had covered up the complainant's 'spy hole', and threatened her. The housing officer then liaised with the police and subsequently maintained close contact on a weekly basis with both the complainant and the tenant who was the subject of the complaint.

The housing officer concluded that the tenant did have a special case for rehousing since he was reportedly petrified of his associates. It seems that he had barricaded the door to his flat and was entering it by climbing from the window in the stairway to his bedroom window via a ledge on the ninth floor. However, the situation was complicated because the tenant in question did not respond to letters. Consequently, communications had to be effected via his mother and sister. At the time of writing up the report both tenants were waiting to move. As in the previous case, there would appear to be little scope for mediation in relation to disputes of this kind.

The housing officer estimated that the case had taken in excess of 12 complete days of housing officers' time. We have calculated that the direct costs involved for this level of input would be in the order of £1,093.70 excluding the cost of making good the damaged windows and also the costs of relocating two sets of neighbours. However, we think that this figure should be treated with caution for the reasons we have explained.

Case history 18[29]

This neighbour nuisance case is principally a result of domestic violence in which the tenant is once again probably at least as much a victim as the neighbours who were also affected by it.[30]

On 16 January 1996, housing officers received a report from a caretaker of a block of flats stating that numerous complaints had been made regarding a particular tenant. The caretaker asked if the officers would visit a neighbour who had befriended the tenant in question. The neighbour reported hearing continuous shouting and banging from the adjoining flat, linked with numerous visits from the police. However she stated that the problems were caused by the tenant's boyfriend, who regularly assaulted her and stole her property. According to the neighbour, the boyfriend was then on bail, but no bail hostel would accept him. She was advised to keep a diary of events, and to ask the tenant to contact the housing officer urgently.

The tenant telephoned the housing officer and stated that her boyfriend had cut her and stolen her giro. She was waiting for the police to arrive. She agreed to the suggestion that she needed to be moved out and rehoused very quickly. The housing officer spent some time liaising with the police, who confirmed the accuracy of the reports, and stated that the tenant was too afraid to proceed with a

prosecution against the boyfriend. She also arranged for emergency accommodation for the tenant at a bail hostel, and spoke with the homeless unit who agreed to organise temporary accommodation for her.

The housing officer phoned the bail hostel the next day, only to discover that the tenant had not spent the night there but instead had returned to her flat. When she spoke to the caretaker a couple of days later the housing officer was told that the boyfriend was staying with the tenant though things had been quiet. When the tenant contacted the housing office it was explained to her that if the problems persisted she risked losing her home.

Just over a week later, a letter of complaint was received from one of the neighbours and, on investigating further, the housing officer was told by the neighbour who had befriended the tenant that while there had been no fighting, there had been arguments and shouting. The housing officer then left diary sheets with four neighbours, all of whom complained of banging, shouting and abusive language day and night. One of the tenants reported that the boyfriend urinated on the walls and also that there was blood on the walls. However they all stated that thing had quietened down over the last week and a half.

The tenant was seen on the following day, and was again warned of the consequences if problems continued. However, she was also offered the chance of being rehoused in view of the violence she had experienced. By March 1996 the problems were escalating again, and on 21 March the police had been called to the flat. By this stage the decision had been taken to seek possession of the flat. The tenant was again offered rehousing, but insisted that she did not want to leave her boyfriend, even though she was afraid of him.

On 29 April, the tenant was served with a notice seeking possession for noise nuisance and rent arrears. She sought the help of a solicitor, and it was explained that if she abided by the tenancy agreement nothing further would happen. Between then and the time the case history was written up (in May 1996) there had been no further problems. However, the elderly couple who lived upstairs from the flat had indicated a desire to move following the disturbance they had experienced.

The housing officer estimated that the case had taken more than 20 full days of housing officer's time. We have calculated that the direct costs involved for this level of input would be in the order of £1,822.84, and we were told that this did not include all of the occasions on which the tenant called into the housing office to discuss her problems since these were not all logged.[31]

Case history 19

The final neighbour nuisance case from area 'c' illustrates the kind of problems that are often associated with attempts to find homes for tenants suffering from mental health problems in line with the 'care in the community' initiative. The brief facts of the dispute, and its effects on those involved have already been recounted briefly in Chapter 5.[32] The problem facing housing officers in this case was that while the tenant whose behaviour was complained of was considered to have mental health problems, he was not sectionable during the course of the tenancy.

Housing officials responded to the complaints initially by sending the tenant a nuisance warning letter, and by investigating the various allegations and counter allegations. In most cases these involved visits to the tenant in question or his neighbours, though many of these proved to be abortive.

Despite the repeated allegations that the tenant was damaging council property, and the extremely anti-social behaviour experienced by many of his neighbours, housing officials found it extremely difficult to obtain satisfactory proof that the tenant in question was responsible for the incidents complained of. At one point the possibility of installing closed circuit security cameras was under consideration, but this was rejected on the ground that there was nowhere they could be sited where they could not be tampered with.

In November 1995, which was about seven months after the complaints had first started, a senior housing officer visited the tenant together with a member of the mental health team, a general practitioner, a consultant psychiatrist and a community police officer, presumably with a view to sectioning the tenant. There was no response when they called, though the police were said to have a warrant ready to sign for psychiatric assessment if there were further disturbances.

Over the following weeks housing officers were in close contact with a number of the residents whose complaints about the effects of the tenant's anti social behaviour were clearly being taken very seriously. During this period also, a number of visits were made by the works department team, and also by electricians, to repair various acts of damage including interference with the main fuses. This damage was said to have severely endangered residents as it presented a serous fire hazard.

At this stage, solicitors acting for one of the residents were informed that the housing office were treating the matter as a mental health issue with a view to seeking a section rather than a case for repossession. In late December 1995 the senior housing officer, GP, a social worker and a consultant psychiatrist again visited the tenant in an attempt to section him. Despite much persuasion the door was not answered, and the team agreed to make another attempt over the Christmas and New Year period, and to go for a warrant on the same day if there was no result.

In early January 1996, the tenant whose behaviour was complained of was involved in a number of threatening incidents. The police attended in response to one of these, together with the tenant's GP and a consultant psychiatrist. The latter apparently stated that there was nothing wrong with A, though the GP later accepted that the tenant did have definite mental health problems.

On 24 January 1996, the tenant's GP convened a meeting about his patient following visits from his neighbours. The meeting was also attended by a senior housing officer, the housing area manager, a social worker, the community constable and a representative of the Racial Equality Council. It was reported that the tenant causing all the problems now wished to move.

By early February 1996 a further meeting of the psychiatric assessment team concluded that the tenant was not sectionable after all, and housing officials began seeking advice from evidence from the police and advice from the legal and administration department with a view to initiating possession proceedings. However, a memo from the area manager to the Director of Housing dated 15

February warned that, as there was no hard evidence against the tenant in question, the legal section had advised that the office would not succeed in taking action against him.

Further attempts were made over the next few weeks to obtain information from the police and also the tenant's GP, while the police and a solicitor acting for one of the residents expressed concern for the latter's safety and sought further action against the tenant. Towards the end of February a case conference was called, only to be rearranged because some of the participants could not make it. At the same time Environmental Services were requested to consider the installation of noise monitoring equipment. Meanwhile, housing officials continued to liaise with the City Solicitor over what steps might be taken to repossess the property.

In early March 1996, matters came to a head when the caretaker of the flats phoned to say that she had seen the tenant in question throw a brick through one of his neighbour's windows while she was in the latter's flat giving a statement to the police. The offending tenant was arrested, and assaulted a police officer in the process. He was held in custody overnight and was remanded on bail until 3 April 1996.

Shortly after this, housing officials sought to arrange for witness statements to be obtained from four of the tenant's neighbours. Towards the end of March, the police provided information relating to the fourteen incidents at which they had been required to attend since the beginning of 1995. By the time the case history was being written up, Environmental Services sent a memo stating that they had received no further details regarding their possible involvement with the problem tenant. However it did appear probable that an action for possession would be sought almost exactly one year after the first complaints were received alleging serious disturbance.

During this period it appears that at least 43.67 hours of housing officers' time had been expended on this one case which had involved officials at every level within the department. We calculate that the direct costs alone in this case amount to £955.92,[33] but even this represents only a fraction of the total cost of the dispute (which was still ongoing), since we have been unable to calculate the cost to the various other agencies involved let alone the substantial repair bills. The toll on the emotional and psychological well-being of the other residents over this period is also incalculable, but constitutes an additional very substantial human cost in addition to the considerable financial expense incurred.

Assessing the scope for savings in relation to the consequential costs of neighbour disputes for social landlords

So far, we have been concentrating on the direct costs that may be incurred by social landlords when dealing with neighbour disputes after a request from one or both parties for them to take action. However, as we explained earlier, and as Figure 6.1 makes clear, these are not the only costs involved, and may not always be the main ones. They also vary considerably in the extent to which they can be reliably quantified.

The easiest of these additional direct costs to quantify are the legal costs that are associated with formal enforcement actions such as applications for possession or injunctions, since the staff employed by administration and legal departments do tend to keep highly accurate records of the amount of time they spend on each case, which is then 'charged' to the Housing Department in the form of overheads. We will examine these costs in greater detail in Chapter 7.

Where neighbour disputes result in a transfer of tenancy (other than a mutual exchange) this is also likely to result in a variety of additional direct costs, some of which will almost certainly have to be borne by the social landlord. They include the cost of repairing any damage to the property that might have been inflicted in the course of a neighbour dispute, cleaning and refurbishing the premises for reletting and protecting any properties that are likely to remain unlet for any period (normally referred to as 'void' properties), since unoccupied premises are often a target for acts of vandalism.

In addition to these direct costs, social landlords are also likely to sustain a variety of indirect costs as a result of some neighbour dispute-related moves. They include a loss of income in respect of properties that are not immediately relet following a relocation, and on estates suffering high levels of anti-social behaviour there may be a risk of longer term revenue loss if this contributes to an increase in the 'void rate'.[34] Another form of indirect cost to social landlords in such circumstances is a reduction in the market value and 'marketability' of housing stock. Indirect costs such as these are particularly difficult to quantify, as are the various 'opportunity costs' referred to in Figure 6.1.

Nevertheless, we have attempted to quantify as many of these additional consequential costs as we were able to within the limitations of the available data. This is necessary in order to estimate the potential scope for savings that might be made on the assumption that it should be possible, at least in certain cases, to avoid the relocation of tenants by relying on mediation instead. In case study 2, below, we consider the extent which it is possible to quantify the costs that might be incurred as a result of neighbour dispute-related moves.

Case study 2

We sought information relating to the cost of neighbour dispute related moves from Councils A and B. Within Council A, the area office serving area 'a' had recently conducted a study investigating the cost to the department of excessive quittings from just five roads in the area which have become notorious for crime and neighbourhood problems. In the 1994 to 1995 financial year there were 57 quittings and 34 Mutual Exchanges on these five roads alone.[35] In the 1995 to 1996 financial year, this had increased to 104 quittings and 9 Mutual Exchanges. The turnover of tenancies had risen from 40% to 50% in a year, and the prospects of finding another tenant willing to exchange into the five roads had been greatly reduced.

In the remainder of the area (i.e. outside of these five roads) there were 516 quittings in the 1995 to 1996 financial year (9.3%). If the five roads had shown the same level of quittings which was normal for the rest of the area, there would have been only 21 quittings throughout the year instead of the 104 that actually took place. In other words, the effects of crime and harassment on the five roads (overwhelmingly the reason given at the time of quitting) produced an extra 83 vacant properties during the year. The housing office estimated that the cost of excessive quittings on these five roads

was £15,000 in 1993/94 and £50,000 in 1995/96.

Most of the indirect costs involved can be assumed to result from rent loss, plus the cost of repairs and security measures which must be taken for vacant properties after the tenant has quit possession. [Where the move takes the form of a mutual exchange, the costs to the Housing Department are normally fairly negligible]. Based on the above estimates, the average cost of these additional quittings was £602.41 per property in 1995/6.

We were able to obtain much more detailed costings from Council B, whose Housing Department has recently introduced a set of key performance indicators. These enable the various costs (including rent loss, cleaning costs, repair costs and number of days void) that contribute to the overall turn-around cost for properties to be more precisely calculated.

We examined the detailed performance indicators relating to twelve sets of properties that had been vacated in a variety of circumstances[36] in Council B's area 'e'. These showed that the average rent loss alone was £483.86 per property. The figures are based on an average 'void period' of 117 days,[37] and a daily rent loss of £4.13. However, in Council B, the rent loss accounted for only approximately 30% of the total turnaround costs. Most of the remainder was attributable to the cost of repairs and refurbishment, but we were informed that such costs were not often incurred where the move was associated with anti social behaviour.

However, one additional cost which is not separately itemised in Council B's performance indicators is the cost of securing the unoccupied premises until they are relet, and also cleaning them. The cost of applying security screens (which in the case of Council A are rented) is £45 per week.[38] Assuming an average void period of just under seventeen weeks per property in Council B, the cost of securing the property against vandalism could add a further £765 per property, making a total of £1,248.86, which is more than twice Council A's estimate.

Having established the average costs associated with a quitting, we set out to ascertain the number of quittings (or other types of tenancy transfer) that could be attributed to neighbour disputes within Council A's area 'a'. While examining the outcomes of the cases dealt with in housing area 'a' during 1994, we identified all cases in which one of the parties appeared to have moved as a direct result of the dispute. We inferred that this was the case if the relevant property file indicated that the tenant was seeking to move because of the dispute and/or if the tenant moved soon after the dispute – unless there was evidence that this was for a reason other than the dispute.

During 1994 there appeared to be sixteen neighbour dispute cases in which the complainant moved, ostensibly as a result of the dispute, and one case in which a tenancy was abandoned. In addition, twelve tenants were transferred with consent, there were six mutual exchanges and a further three tenants gave notice to quit.

On 1 June 1995, a new recording system was introduced in Council A's housing department which enables the number of 'special transfers' to be identified, almost all of which are neighbour nuisance cases (though as we have seen, neighbour disputes can also give rise to other types of tenancy transfer). This shows that between 1 April 1995 and 31 March 1996 there were a total of 19 special transfers to properties in area 'a'.[39]

During the period in which we conducted our case study in area 'a' the procedure for processing special cases was based on a special case report which was written by the management officer and took approximately one day of his time to collate the information and complete the report. Special cases were then assessed at a half-day meeting attended by area managers from four of the housing areas in Council A. Up to 6 or 8 special cases night be considered in such meetings. If the meeting decided to award the case special priority for rehousing a letter would be sent to the tenant informing them, and they would then enter the rehousing procedure to be dealt with as for all other allocations. Taking into account the time involved, we have estimated that the additional cost involved in preparing and processing such cases could be as much as £141.44.[40]

If we assume that there are approximately 20 cases a year in area 'a' in which tenants are either involved in special transfers or abandon their tenancy as a direct result of neighbour disputes, and if we assume that the average turnaround cost for these properties within Council A[41] is about £602,

the total cost incurred as a result could be as much as £12,040.[42] Moreover, this does not take into account any reduction in the market value of the properties on an estate that might occur when problems such as intractable neighbour disputes, harassment and growing levels of crime result in a downward spiral in the reputation of an area.

Finally, the area office staff in area 'a' also indicated that neighbour nuisance is taking up more and more of Management Officer's time, quite apart from the problem of increased property turnover. This presents other hidden costs: because staff are spending more time on neighbour nuisance they have less time for dealing with other matters such as rent arrears, as a result of which the amount of money owed to the department in rent arrears has also increased. Unfortunately, we were unable to quantify these particular opportunity costs.

Although we cannot precisely quantify all of the indirect costs involved, case study 2 suggests that where social landlords do respond to neighbour disputes by moving one of the parties (unless by way of mutual exchange) this is likely to result in a considerable additional expense on top of the direct salary costs.[43] This obviously needs to be borne in mind when assessing the potential scope for savings in cases that can be successfully resolved by means of mediation.

In addition, various other direct costs might also be incurred as a result of neighbour disputes, whether or not housing officers are asked to intervene. For example, in the course of our case studies we became increasingly conscious of the fact that caretakers and direct works staff may also spend a considerable amount of their time dealing with the consequences of neighbour disputes, particularly where these have resulted in damage to council property. It is much more difficult to ascertain how much of their time might be devoted to individual disputes since any information relating to their involvement is much less likely to be recorded in the relevant housing files.

However, we were able to make a rough estimate of the annual bill for the repair of property damage that might be attributable to neighbour nuisance cases, again in relation to area 'a' in Council A, as we explain in case study 3, below.

Case study 3

We asked the Housing Department in Council A to provide us with the total amount spent on repairing property damage, including vandalism, for each of the four areas we had worked with for the financial years 1994/5 and 1995/6, and to estimate how much of this might be attributable to neighbour nuisance-related incidents. The results are shown in Table 6.3.

The recorded repair costs for area 'a' amounted to £5,263 in 1994/5 and £6,276 in 1995/6. These figures are considerably less than the average for all four areas, which came to £14,103 in 1994/5 and £16,241 in 1995/6. The reason for the disparity is that the recorded repair cost for one of the areas (area 'b' which recorded £41,685 of property repairs in 1995/6) was out of line with all the others.[44] This suggests either that the amount of property damage varies considerably from area to area or that some housing areas are more diligent in recording and accurately coding the repair costs than others.

The number of repair jobs in area 'a' was estimated to be 103 in 1994/5 and 123 in 1995/6, which gives an average price per repair of just over £51.00. However, this figure is somewhat misleading since it relates to the number of visits made rather than the number of properties repaired.[45] If it is assumed that approximately one quarter of the total number of repairs consists of return visits, the number of properties sustaining damage in 1995/6 could be around 92, with an average cost per property of about £68.22.

However, not all of the property damage is attributable to neighbour nuisance cases. We were informed that this would be true of approximately half of the repair costs, which would be equivalent to £3,138 for area 'a' in 1995/6 (and over £20,000 for area 'b'). Not all the neighbour nuisance cases resulting in property damage would necessarily be suitable for mediation. Moreover, some of the costs might be recouped, if necessary by taking court action against those responsible.

Table 6.3: Cost of repairing property damage in study areas.

Area	1994/5		1995/6	
	Expenditure	No. of repairs (estimated)	Expenditure	No. of repairs (actual)
'a'	£5,263	103	£6,276	123
'b'	£37,393	659	£41,685	791
'c'	£3,972	119	£5,554	166
'd'	£9,241	205	£11,652	258

Quantifying the total cost of neighbour disputes for housing departments

It should be clear by now that neighbour disputes inflict a variety of costs on social landlords, only some of which are directly attributable to their role as 'intermediaries' in the dispute. The most easily quantified of these are the direct salary and associated costs relating to the time spent by housing officers dealing with the dispute. As we have seen, these can vary tremendously from case to case, and while the overall average may appear to be relatively modest, a small minority of cases prove very time consuming and expensive to deal with. A second set of costs we have identified are those that arise when one of the parties to a dispute is moved, in an attempt to resolve the problem.

However, the cost of intervention is only part of the picture. As we have seen, neighbour disputes also generate a range of additional costs for social landlords whether or not they are called upon to intervene in a dispute. One such cost is the expense of repairing damage to property that is sustained as a result of acts of neighbour nuisance. Although not all of these consequential costs can be quantified with any degree of precision, and in spite of the fact that they are likely to vary considerably from case to case, these should not be overlooked in any attempt to estimate the potential savings that might be achieved if more effective ways can be found for dealing with neighbour disputes. This is an issue we will return to in Chapter 9.

Meanwhile, we are now in a position to calculate the combined neighbour dispute costs that were sustained by a single housing department over a twelve month period insofar as these can be quantified. This calculation is based on the sum of the costs

Table 6.4: Assessing the total cost of neighbour disputes as sustained by a single urban housing area over a twelve month period

Type of cost incurred	Amount
Direct salary and related costs incurred as a result of informal action	5764.10
Cost associated with moving one of the parties to a dispute	12040.00
Cost of repairing property damage resulting from neighbour nuisance	3138.00
Total costs	20942.10

Source of data: case studies 1-3 based on Council A, housing area 'a'

we identified in case studies 1, 2 and 3, and is set out in Table 6.4.

As can be seen, the total cost that could reasonably be attributed to neighbour nuisance and its consequences in respect of a single housing area within Council A over a twelve month period was at least £20,942. If representative, this figure would need to be multiplied by the number of housing areas within a council to arrive at a global figure for the council as a whole. In respect of Council A, the total cost assessed on this basis would probably be in excess of £310,000.

Finally, neighbour disputes may give rise to various 'external costs' (see Figure 6.1), many of which are difficult or impossible to quantify: as in the case of the emotional or psychological effects on the parties and their families, or on the staff who have to deal with the disputes. It should also be noted that while some of these costs may be 'external' to the Housing Department, they may still fall on other council departments such as social services. One example we came across in a number of cases relates to the cost of fumigating or thoroughly cleansing a property, which is likely to be borne by either the environmental health or social services department.

In the next chapter, we attempt to quantify the costs that might be incurred in respect of the relatively small proportion of cases that involve more formal legal interventions of various kinds.

Notes

1 Bearing in mind the need to ensure that 'like' is being compared with 'like'. This would not be the case if the other consequential costs, such as those relating to the cost of repairing property damage, were also incorporated into the equation since they are not directly related to the social landlord's role as intermediary.

2 These are the costs we will mainly refer to in Chapter 9 when seeking to compare the cost of mediation with the cost of informal interventions by social landlords.

3 In just the same way that other agencies such as the police or environmental services could also be expected to benefit from consequential savings if neighbour disputes could be dealt with more effectively.

4 Assuming the issue of confidentiality can be successfully resolved. We were only provided with sufficiently detailed information to be able to make these calculations in respect of Councils A and B.

5 The survey included all neighbour nuisance cases on which action was taken during the period 1st January 1994 and 31 December 1994. Where a case commenced before January 1994 or continued beyond December 1994 there would be other actions outside the relevant time period, but these have not been included in the survey.

6 Fortunately, area 'a' had undertaken its own time monitoring exercise during 1994, to which we were given access.

7 See Chapter 9.

8 And also the findings of the time-monitoring exercise relating to the same period, which had been conducted by area 'a' housing office staff.

9 Two visits were made in 18% of cases, and three or more visits were made in 9.4% of cases.

10 No accurate records had been kept of the number of referrals to the local independent mediation service, but staff estimated that in the six month period between April and September 1995 there had been approximately 20 per month.

11 Salaries plus overheads.

12 Internal report to Council A's Nuisance Working Party.

13 Their costs would not have been covered by the time monitoring exercise, and consequently do not appear in our own calculations either.

14 One such exercise was conducted over a four week period in November 1993. Another covered an eight week period in spring 1994.

15 See Appendix 2 for details; column headed Hours per Annum: Neighbour Nuisance Prop'n.

16 For example in case history 19 (see page 55, below), which was dealt with in Council A's housing area 'd', the expenditure over a twelve month period was at least £955.92

17 Within the limitations of the data. In some cases we were aware that not every action had been recorded. Some files only contained details of the main events and actions and most of them excluded time spent writing up reports, informal consultations with colleagues within the department and some telephone calls. Almost certainly, therefore, the costs we have calculated will have a tendency to somewhat underestimate the true economic cost of the dispute for the department or office concerned.

18 We have not attempted to make any provision for time or financial resources expended by other council departments such as Environmental Services or City Solicitors, nor agencies such as the police or Local Government Ombudsman.

19 Indeed, this view appears to have been taken in at least two of the case histories selected from this area, though in the event neither case was resolved in this way.

20 As we have explained above, all case histories are numbered sequentially for ease of identification.

21 At least initially. In this and some of the other cases involving criminal activity which we will be examining, one response to the criminal behaviour of some of those involved might be to attempt to mediate between offender and victim(s) with a view to securing reparation for some or all of those affected though not all community mediation services are involved with mediation of this kind.

22 Unlike the housing department in Council B, which not only acts on complaints by owner occupiers against council tenants, but also in respect of complaints by tenants against either private tenants or owner occupiers, at least where the properties concerned are covered by the 'right to buy' legislation.

23 Case history 19, on page 55, illustrates the kind of neighbour dispute that can be associated with such cases and the problems they pose for social landlords. See also case histories 5 and 6 above.

24 Because the dispute had lasted so long the annualised case cost was relatively small at £45.90.

25 See above, page 47.

26 Interestingly, tenant X was also the boyfriend who initially held part of the tenancy in the dispute described in case history 12 above (see page 47ff). Only the main actions and events are recorded here.

27 This figure should be treated with caution. Compared with areas 'a' and 'b', some of the case files in area 'c' were less detailed, and in some cases housing officers were only to give 'global estimates' of the time spent on the whole case and were unable to quantify the time spent on specific tasks. This approach is likely to over-estimate the time actually spent.

28 Unfortunately, not all the actions in the case were logged on the housing file, and as a result, only the main events have been chronicled in the case history. However, the amount of time spent is based on a 'global' estimate, as in the previous case, and a similar 'health warning' therefore applies to it also.

29 See also case history 7 in chapter 5 (p. 37), since we have used this same case to illustrate some of the unquantifiable human costs (both for the disputant and others) that neighbour disputes all too often give rise to.

30 As with the above case, not all actions and events were logged in the housing file, so the account only covers the main episodes and actions. Once again the effect is likely to depress to some extent the estimated time and costs involved.

31 However the calculation is based on a global estimate of the amount of time spent on the case, and therefore the same 'health warning' applies as to the previous two cases.

32 See case history 5 on page 35 above.

33 Another care in the community case (case history 6, which we referred to in Chapter 5 in order to illustrate the human and social costs to which neighbour disputes can give rise) was also estimated to have cost the area office concerned (area 'd'') £902.30 over a period of 5.4 years.

34 Meaning the proportion of properties for which tenants cannot be found.

35 Not all of these would have been directly attributable to ongoing neighbour disputes, however.

36 These include abandonments, transfers and special circumstances where the tenant's application to move is granted without insisting on a mutual exchange. Once again, not all of these are necessarily the result of neighbour disputes. Nevertheless they do indicate the potential costs to the landlord when properties do fall vacant for whatever reason.

37 This compares with an average turnaround period in Council A's area 'a' of 55.6 days during the period of our case study, resulting in a rent loss of just under 8 weeks.

38 An alternative but rarely used method (in Council A) involves the application of timber boarding which costs £515 per property to erect and £206 to remove.

39 Some of these could have come from outside the area; conversely, some area 'a' tenants may have moved to other areas under the 'special cases' procedure. Unfortunately the new recording system cannot trace such cases back to their area of origin, which is where most of the costs associated with preparing the transfer would have been incurred.

40 Based on the appropriate hourly rates plus overheads for the grades of staff involved.

41 As we have seen, the estimated turnaround costs for Council B are very much higher at £1,249 per property.

42 This greatly exceeds the total cost of all informal interventions by area 'a' housing staff in respect of all 117 cases in which they took action in 1994 which, as we saw earlier, was costed at only £5,764.10.

43 Moreover, there can be no guarantee that moving one of the parties will resolve the problem, since in some cases the dispute may flare up again with a different set of protagonists..

44 In 1994/5 the figure of £37,393 was four times greater than the recorded repair costs for the second highest area, and in 1995/6 the figure of £41,685 was three times greater than for the second highest area.

45 For example, where a window is broken at night a temporary repair is effected by installing a window board. When the window is subsequently glazed, this counts as a second repair.

Assessing the costs of formal action involving housing and legal services

Introduction: Aims and Methods

In the previous chapter we were only concerned with the resource costs that might be incurred by housing services in respect of neighbour disputes that are dealt with informally. Numerically this accounts for the vast majority of all cases that are handled by housing departments. However, it seems probable that for those few cases that involve legal interventions of one form or another, the total costs that are incurred may be considerable since they will also include payment for any legal advice or support that may be required. Consequently, the scope for any financial savings may also be greater where such action can be avoided.

In this chapter we attempt to quantify the combined housing and legal service costs that might be involved in respect of a range of formal legal interventions as follows:

- where legal services are involved but only in an advisory capacity;

- where an injunction is sought;

- where a notice to seek possession (NSP) is sought or obtained; and

- where an eviction is obtained.

Once again our analysis is mainly based on a series of 'case histories'. We have selected these from cases dealt with over the last two years in another urban local authority – Council B – which is also situated in the north of England. Council B was selected partly because of the quality of its record-keeping, and also its willingness to participate in the research, but mainly because it has a much more vigorous enforcement policy compared with Councils A and C.

For each case history we have attempted to undertake a 'cradle-to-grave' cost analysis covering all the direct revenue and associated costs incurred by both housing and administrative and legal services from the first intervention in a neighbour dispute to the completion of any legal action. In order to ascertain the costs to Council B's Housing Department, we examined the relevant property file and itemised every action relating to the dispute. The officers concerned were then asked to estimate how long each action took to complete.

The method used to calculate the cost to the Legal and Admin Department was essentially the same except that the billing procedure was based on continuous electronic time monitoring which automatically recorded both the time taken for every action and also the cost involved, which greatly facilitated the task of data collection.

It might be objected that such an exercise involves an element of double-counting since some of these costs will in fact be 'charged' to housing, and will appear as an element in their overheads.

While this is probably correct in terms of a strict cost-benefit approach, it runs the risk of obscuring the scale of savings that might be attainable if even very small numbers of cases that currently end up in court could be dealt with instead by way of mediation. Indeed, the issue highlights a more general methodological problem concerning the matter of overheads when seeking to establish a 'level playing field' between mediation services and local authority housing departments.

The problem arises when seeking to compare small-scale organisations such as community mediation services, which have only one or at most two main spheres of activity, with very much larger organisations such as council departments engaged in a vast range of different activities. With the former, all the relevant overheads are chargeable to just one or two main service areas, and thus account for a relatively large proportion of the total costs.

However, because neighbour dispute work forms only a tiny proportion of the total activities pursued by local authority housing departments,

Figure 7.1: Involvement of Legal and Admin Services for Council B in neighbour dispute cases

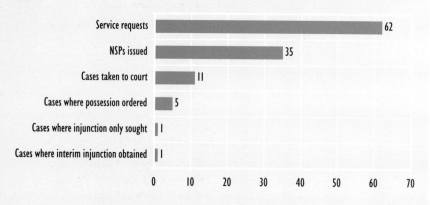

Source of data: case study based on formal interventions undertaken by Council B

property is involved than where the complaints relates solely to noise nuisance.

In 1995-6, Council B dealt with a total of 821 disputes, of which 164 were brought forward from the previous year, while 657 were new cases. During this period, a total of 110 Notices of intention to Seek Possession (NSPs) were issued, 23 injunctions or court orders were sought and 8 tenants were evicted. Figure 7.1 gives a more detailed picture of the extent to which, compared with many other councils including Council A, the legal and administration department in Council B is relatively actively involved in the handling of neighbour nuisance cases.

Of the 62 service requests received by the Legal and Admin Department, Notices of intention to Seek Possession were issued in respect of 35 tenants. Eleven of these were taken to court, and five resulted in possession being ordered in favour of the council. In one of the cases an injunction only was sought. In 26 cases the department was involved in an advisory capacity only, and in one case an interim injunction was obtained. The use of injunctions and temporary injunctions by the council follows a recent internal review in which it was decided that possession was not always the most appropriate remedy.

it bears only a minute share of the overall overheads. It is in this sense that the additional legal costs that are associated with neighbour dispute work might get obscured by treating them simply as part of the department's overheads.[1] This is why we have felt it necessary to supplement the housing department costings with a number of illustrative case histories.[2]

As in the previous chapter, we have not attempted to make any provision for time or financial resources expended by other council departments such as Environmental Services or Social Services, nor by agencies such as the police, the courts (including the legal aid fund) or Local Government Ombudsman. Nor have we attempted to include any of the 'hidden' or indirect costs that might be involved.

Putting the study in context: Council B's policy on neighbour nuisance

Council officers describe Council B's policy in relation to neighbour nuisance complaints as 'firm but fair'. There is support for mediation in principle, and the local mediation service is said to be well used, but at the same time housing and legal officers do not hesitate to bring legal proceedings where this is considered to be appropriate. One reason we were given for the Housing Department's more proactive policy (when compared with that of the Environmental Health Department, for example) is that there is felt to be more at stake where the council's

Assessing the cost of formal intervention by local authority housing departments

For this part of the research we again worked closely with one local area housing office, though this time in Council B. The tenure profile for area 'e' comprises 86% Local Authority dwellings, 13.2% owner occupied dwellings and 0.8% privately rented dwellings. The local authority housing comprises 509 houses, 75 bungalows, 51 purpose-built flats or maisonettes and one bed-sit.

The area has an unemployment rate of 23% which is twice that of the borough as a whole. The estate has a predominantly white population (98%). The estate suffers from a combination of anti-social behaviour, drugs and crime problems. Because of its reputation, properties are difficult to let and it has a high 'void rate'.

The following case histories have been selected to illustrate the costs that are likely to be incurred where neighbour disputes give rise to various kinds of formal intervention involving both housing services and also legal and administration departments.

Case history 20: Legal and Admin involved but only in an advisory capacity

In this case the complaints were about noise nuisance from Tenant A, caused by shouting, banging doors and loud music. Most of the noise appeared to be due to visitors. The complaints began in July 1995, and diary sheets were given to two sets of neighbours (Tenants B and C). Tenant A was visited (three times) and was reminded of her tenancy obligations.

When the complaints persisted, the Legal and Admin department was contacted (in November 1995) for advice in relation to the serving of a Notice to Seek Possession. The tenant explained that the noise was made by unwelcome guests and was warned of the consequences unless the situation improved.

In February 1996, diary sheets were received from Tenant C complaining of noise nuisance during the period covering 24 July 1995 to 15 February 1996. The Assistant Estate Manager made a request for legal proceedings to be commenced due to continuing noise nuisance, but a note attached to the request asked for a memo to be sent to the legal section to delay the NSP as the nuisance appeared to have been resolved.

The total time spent by the housing department amounted to 4.6 hours, at a cost of £158.58, in addition to which the Legal and Admin department spent four hours on the case which was costed at £132.00, making a total of £290.58.

Case history 21: Granting of injunction

This rather unusual neighbour dispute arose as a result of complaints from neighbours that the tenant in question was not allowing access to the property in an area that had been designated for improvement under the Estates Action programme. Consequently, the neighbours were suffering because work on their properties could not commence.

Although the tenant was believed to be in breach of the tenancy agreement by not allowing access, it was considered inappropriate to go for possession proceedings, and the council decided to apply for an injunction instead. This was granted, enabling the work to proceed. Even though this was not a conventional neighbour dispute, the cost to the council of obtaining the injunction was felt to be typical and came to £898.15 for 27 hours and 9 minutes work.[3]

Case history 22: Notice of Intention to Seek Possession issued but not enforced

In this dispute, allegations of noise and other forms of nuisance were made against a particular tenant by at least four neighbours. The complaints started almost as soon as the tenant moved into her property, in June 1995. The noise nuisance was mainly caused by people visiting the property at all hours of the day and night. It was suspected that the tenant may be dealing in drugs, and she was in fact arrested for drug dealing.

Early in July 1995, both next door neighbours complained to the Housing Office about men coming and going at high speed in cars, kicking the front door and verbally abusing the tenant. In August 1995 it was reported to the Housing Office that the tenant had been arrested, reportedly for drug dealing. Enquiries with the police revealed that the tenant had convictions for shoplifting and motoring offences, but to date had no convictions for drug offences.

After a number of further complaints and diary sheets which reported noise nuisance caused by visitors, loud music and visitors trespassing across other tenants' gardens, a Notice Seeking Possession was served on the tenant at the end of November 1995. No further nuisances were reported, but then in January 1996 the tenant was arrested for drug dealing. As a consequence, the Housing Department asked the Legal and Admin Department to commence legal proceedings against the tenant. However, the latter advised that as the tenant had been arrested from a different address this could not be used in possession proceedings.

Following her arrest, the tenant lost her job and lived temporarily elsewhere. On returning to her home, the noise nuisance did not resume and the Housing Office decided to drop the possession proceedings on grounds of anti-social behaviour, though they continued to pursue a suspended possession order on grounds of rent arrears.

Throughout the course of the dispute four letters were sent to the alleged perpetrator, there were four telephone calls from complainants, and a letter from a complainant. There were also five visits or interviews with complainants, and five with the alleged perpetrator. In addition there was some correspondence between the Housing Department and the legal section. The case is estimated to have consumed 12.67 hours of housing staff time at an estimated direct cost of £449.27.

In addition to this, the time spent on the case by Council B's Legal and Admin Department (solely in relation to the anti social behaviour) amounted to 7 hours 43 minutes and was costed at £254.65, making a total of £703.92.

Case history 23: Notice of Intention to Seek Possession issued but not enforced

This was a case involving complaints about noise nuisance and disruption caused by severe domestic disturbances. The first complaints were received in April 1995 and concerned loud music and a disturbance caused by Tenant A's boyfriend, to which the police were called. The complaints persisted during the summer, and in one incident in July 1995 one of Tenant A's neighbours (Tenant B) complained of disturbances lasting throughout the night, and of her partner wielding a knife in the street. Subsequently someone was stabbed, and again the police were called.

Tenant B explained that Tenant A's ex-husband had kicked the door down and stabbed a man who was at her house. Later in the year another neighbour reported a further incident in

which the police arrested a man from Tenant A's address, and a woman ran down the street after the police. She reported that a gang of youths had broken all the windows at the house, and that she could no longer cope with the comings and goings.

In December 1995, a senior legal assistant wrote to the Assistant Estate Manager enclosing a Notice of Intention to Seek Possession and advising that because neighbours were reluctant to act as witnesses it might be helpful to call a case conference. This would enable the burden of proof to be discussed, and would clarify that the council is virtually powerless to act on its own. The Notice was served on the following day.

In April 1996 further complaints were received, following which Tenant A was warned that the council was considering court action which could result in her losing her home. There was a further complaint alleging loud music and fighting in July 1996, and complaints about possible child abuse and further noise nuisance in the following month. Tenant A was given a final warning at this point.

Following further allegations of child abuse the police were called, and social services took the child into care. Tenant A was warned that the Legal Department had been instructed to apply to the courts for an eviction order. A week later her windows were broken, the police were informed and the damage repaired. Shortly afterwards, Tenant A reported that the front windows had again been broken, and offensive graffiti had been written on the front door which accused her of child abuse and threatened her life.

At this point, the threat of legal proceedings was called off, the police were informed and Tenant A was referred to Homeless Welfare for rehousing. The case had involved a total of 13.5 hours of housing officer time at a cost of £467.09. In addition, the Legal and Admin department spent 2¼ hours on the case at a cost of £77.55, making a total of £544.64. The cost of police and social service involvement is not known.

Case history 24: Possession awarded in favour of council

In this dispute complaints were made about the large number of animals belonging to a tenant's adult daughter. There were said to be 17 dogs (including 4 Great Danes), 4 Persian cats in cages and a number of cats which ran free. The family had occupied the house since September 1991, though in practice the daughter lived on her own with the animals at the property, which was a three bedroomed house. The actual tenants, her parents, primarily lived elsewhere.

The complaints came principally from the next door neighbours, a couple who had lived at their property since August 1994. There were also a few complaints from another tenant. Specifically the complaints were about intimidation and noise nuisance from the daughter's many dogs; the erection of an unsightly fence and cat run; and strong disinfectant smells, as well as the run off of disinfectant onto the next door neighbour's garden.

The problems really started in February 1995 when the next door neighbours and neighbours which adjoined the rear of the property complained that the dogs were frightening people. The dog's owner offered to raise the fencing around the property. This appeased the neighbours at the rear of the property, but not the next door neighbours who apparently broke down the fencing one evening. The police were called to this incident but no action was taken.

The next door neighbours' main complaint was about the strong disinfectant used to wash out the dog runs twice daily. They also complained that this disinfectant ran off onto their garden. The owner of the dogs refused to compromise on the type of disinfectant used.

There was also much argument about the type of fence to be erected between the properties. The owner of the dogs initially wanted a totally concrete fence, while the next door neighbours wanted a normal 'waneylap' fence. After inspection and consultation, the Housing Department proposed that two concrete slabs topped off with 'waneylap' might be a reasonable compromise but specifically asked for work not to proceed until both parties had agreed to it. Despite being asked to wait, the owners of the dogs erected a fence which included more concrete than the proposed compromise and was topped off with unsightly timber boards.

During the course of the dispute there was some suggestion that the next door neighbours may not be entirely innocent in that they were accused of provoking the dogs. While the dog owners stated they had witnesses to this, they never provided the names of any witnesses although one neighbour did tell the housing office that she had seen the next door neighbour provoking the dogs.

Six months into the dispute, the dog owners enquired about the possibility of mediation, but as the complainant had seemingly refused to go along with the suggestion, this proposal was not pursued.

In the end, possession of the dog owners' property was granted by the County Court in December 1994 on grounds of nuisance. After two adjournments to the eviction date amid complaints from the tenants that they should still be allowed to continue with their 'Right To Buy' application, the tenants were finally evicted from the property in March 1996. The Council refused to rehouse them as they had made themselves intentionally homeless through their anti-social behaviour and were deemed not to be in priority need.

The eviction did not mark the end of the matter as the family complained to the Local Government Ombudsman. The Ombudsman's enquiries were closed after a brief investigation as the Ombudsman decided that the complaints had been satisfactorily dealt with by the Court when it considered the proceedings for eviction.

Throughout the course of the dispute, 18 letters were written to the perpetrators, two to the complainants and three to MPs or Councillors. There were five telephone conversations with the complainants and four with the dog owners, and there were eleven interviews with the complainants and twelve with the dog owners. Environmental Services were involved and there was some contact between them and the Housing Department.. There was also obviously a considerable amount of communication between the Housing Department and Legal Services. In total the dispute consumed an estimated 62.3 hours of Housing staff time at an estimated direct cost of £2,419.42.

The case also involved a considerable amount of Legal and Admin time, resulting in a massive bill of £2,713.70 for the $82^{1}/4$ hours work. The total cost of the dispute for both sets of departments amounted to £5,133.12.

Substantial as they undoubtedly are, the combined costs to the housing and legal and admin departments in cases such as these do not represent the total cost to the public purse, particularly where the tenant contests the proceedings and is granted legal aid. Legal officers for Council B estimated that approximately half the neighbour nuisance possession proceedings are contested.

Where this is the case, the sums involved are likely to be even greater, given that the fees charged by solicitors in private practice are between two and three times greater than the council's solicitors own fees of £30 per hour. Many who contest the proceedings[4] brief counsel, which would involve a minimum fee of £250, and often considerably more. Even these costs do not take into account the full costs of a court action, since they do not include the costs of running the court and paying the salaries of judges and other court officials.

It seems likely that even some of the cases that are currently dealt with by means of formal methods of enforcement might potentially have been mediatable. However, as we have seen, this approach requires consent by both parties. In the eviction case which we examined above, the complainant was unwilling to go along with this; though in other respects the case does not appear to raise any issues that might have precluded the use of mediation. One policy issue that is raised by this and other similar cases is whether more can be done to encourage disputants to give mediation a try, particularly in view of the heavy costs that are involved in legal proceedings.

Lawyers who worked for Council B's Legal and Administration Department and local area housing officials expressed support for the principle of mediation and explained that the local mediation service is well used. However, they explained that because there are insufficient volunteer mediators there may be delays of three to four weeks before mediation can be attempted. Consequently, housing officers are reluctant to refer potentially suitable cases, and the council solicitor admitted that they still received cases (albeit a minority) that should have been resolved informally. All agreed that if mediation is to work, it is essential to get in quickly and early to take the heat out of the situation, and this requires sufficient capacity on the part of the mediation service to cope with the number of referrals.

Notes

1 We are not advocating that such costs should be counted twice; merely that any additional scope for savings that might be achieved if mediation can be successfully used as an alternative to court action should be separately quantified.

2 It would be extremely difficult to ascertain the 'average' costs involved since relatively few cases get as far court action, and those that do differ greatly in their complexity and the way they are handled. Nevertheless, we believe that the cases we have selected are reasonably typical and help to illustrate the scale of costs that might be involved.

3 Unfortunately we were unable to gain access to the property file for this case, so we have not been able to calculate the combined housing and legal costs involved.

4 We were told that as many as two thirds of those contesting the court proceedings also instruct a barrister.

Assessing the cost of neighbour disputes for environmental health services

Introduction: general approach and methods used

As part of our overall cost analysis, we also set out to investigate the cost of dealing with neighbour disputes for the other major local authority department with responsibilities in this area: Environmental Health. For this part of the study we undertook a detailed examination of all domestic noise cases recorded over a 12 month period by the Environmental Services Department located within Council A. Environmental Services have a wide range of responsibilities, as can be seen from Figure 8.1. Not all of these have to do with neighbour disputes, as in the case of requests for pest control services or drainage problems.

We decided to concentrate on domestic noise cases because the vast majority of these do involve neighbour complaints. Other types of complaint that may be referred to Environmental Services such as rubbish dumping, domestic smoke and dog fouling may or may not involve neighbour disputes and, in the case of the latter two categories at least, are much less numerous. Some complaints about animals may also involve neighbour disputes, but as many more of them relate to stray dogs we did not include this category in our survey. Unfortunately, neighbour nuisance complaints tend not to be recorded as a separate category by Environmental Services. It is therefore almost impossible to ascertain precisely how many non noise-related neighbour disputes there are, how they are dealt with or how long they take.

In relation to these domestic noise cases we used two methods for calculating the 'unit costs' involved, each of which has its advantages and draw-backs. Method A was based on a time-monitoring exercise carried out in the Environmental Services department during the twelve month period (1 April 1993 and 31 March 1994) preceding our own investigation. Essentially, this involved a 'top-down' approach in which the proportion of departmental time devoted to domestic noise cases was calculated and applied to the overall departmental budget including all the relevant administrative overheads.

Method B was based on an analysis we undertook of all domestic noise cases originating during the following financial year (1 April 1994 to 31 March 1995) where action was taken that went beyond the sending out of a standard pro forma response. The latter consists of a letter (known as a 'DN1 letter') which outlines departmental policy and explains how to make a formal complaint. By examining individual case files in this way we attempted to 'build up' the costs involved in such cases by estimating the time taken to complete the actions and events that were recorded.

The advantage of Method A is that since time spent was categorised by type of complaint rather than by specific tasks, it may be more comprehensive in some respects, since it is more likely to include ancillary activities such as report-writing and informal consultation with colleagues which are normally omitted from case files. Moreover, provision was also made for 'general office time', by incorporating a factor for time not otherwise spent on specific tasks. This was then apportioned proportionately amongst the various activity areas.

Unit costs calculated in this way are likely to be more comprehensive than those calculated by aggregating costs according to the estimated time spent on those specific case-related activities which are recorded. Apart from the obvious risk of omissions resulting from poor or selective record-keeping, the details that are included in case reports will normally exclude the ancillary activities mentioned above, and possibly also other events. For example, it is likely that not all telephone calls will be logged. In addition, the latter excludes any provision for general office time. It is to be expected, therefore, that there will be a discrepancy between the two sets

LIVERPOOL JOHN MOORES UNIVERSITY
LEARNING SERVICES

Figure 8.1: Break-down of service requests involving Environmental Health in 1993-4 by category of complaint.

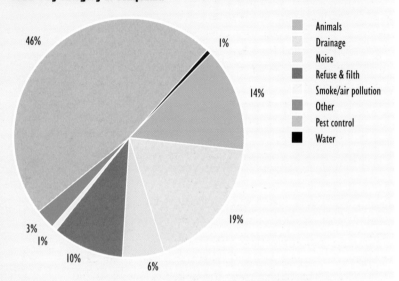

Source of data: Mediation research project case study based on Council A's Environmental Services Department

of calculations, and that the costs derived from Method A could be considerably higher than those derived from Method B.

However, the latter method makes it possible, at least in principle, to calculate the costs incurred in respect of different levels of input; for cases that are dealt with in different ways; and also according to outcome. Consequently, the latter measure may be more useful when seeking to compare the costs and effectiveness of cases dealt with by way of mediation as opposed to more traditional informal or formal measures, despite its tendency to under-estimate the overall costs involved.

Impact of neighbour disputes on Environmental Health Service costs as measured on the basis of a time monitoring approach

During 1993-4, a time monitoring exercise was conducted within the Environmental Services Department in Council A. As can be seen from Figure 8.1, complaints relating to noise, refuse, smoke and other matters accounted for 20% of the total number of service requests handled by the department. The total cost for dealing with these complaints was assessed at £150,560. Allowing 3%

for inflation since then would bring this to £155,076 in 1994/5 prices.

Within this group of complaint categories, complaints about domestic noise accounted for 30% of the total number of complaints.[1] The cost of dealing with domestic noise complaints during this period (assuming the costs of dealing with each category of complaint is approximately the same) was therefore:

155,076 x 30% = £46,523.

A total of 846 domestic noise cases were dealt with, giving an average cost per case of £54.99.

This figure includes all type of noise cases, irrespective of the way they are dealt with. The different types of noise cases and their respective frequencies are shown in Figure 8.2. Although the great majority fall into the category of 'other domestic noise', which accounts for 67% of all noise complaints, over one quarter of these relate to noise from barking dogs, and 6% relate to noise from burglar alarms. Nearly all the 'other domestic noise' complaints could probably be classed as 'neighbour nuisance' cases though it seems likely that a much smaller proportion of the other two types of noise complaints would fall into this category. Moreover there are some differences in the way the different types of noise cases are dealt with.

This is particularly true of dog complaints, which are handled differently to other forms of domestic noise. People complaining of other domestic noise are normally sent a DN1 standard response letter through the post, and only receive a visit if they complete the diaries they are sent and persist in their complaints.[2] In the case of barking dog complaints, however, the complainant always receives a visit by the dog warden, who gives the DN1 to the complainant. In addition, one response that tends to be used only in respect of barking dog cases (and even then only occasionally, since it is not strictly in line with council policy) is to send the person who is being complained about an informal letter (known as a DN2), informing them that a complaint has been received.[3]

It should be noted, also, that the average cost per case of £54.99 includes the very large number of complaints in respect of which the only response is to send a standard form letter involving no further action on the part of the department. The Director of Environmental Services believed that only approximately 20% of complaints went beyond the DN1 stage, and that these cases involved on average around three hours work. He further believed that around 5% of the domestic noise cases that go beyond the DN1 stage are 'extreme' and involve a considerable amount of work.

Impact of neighbour disputes on Environmental Health Service costs as measured by detailed 'case analysis'

The other way of calculating the average cost per case involves analysing the individual files relating to all cases in which action was taken that goes beyond sending a DN1 letter. We did this in respect of all domestic noise cases that appeared to involve neighbour nuisance complaints and which were recorded during the period 1 April 1994 and 31 March 1995.

One of the main advantages of our alternative method of assessing the cost of domestic noise complaints is that it enables the way domestic noise cases are dealt with to be calculated with a much greater degree of precision, and also to determine the relative costs of different levels of intervention.

A total of 848 domestic noise complaints were recorded during this period. Forty two of these did not appear to involve disputes with neighbours,[4] and so were excluded from the analysis. Of the 806 remaining cases, 623 appeared to go no further than a DN1.[5] This is equivalent to 77.3%. Consequently, only around one in five domestic noise complaints were pursued and involved some form of action on the part of Council A's Environmental Services department, which is closely in line with the Director's estimate.

Unfortunately, of the 183 cases that were recorded on the computer as involving further action of some kind, no trace could be found of the paper file relating to 51 of these cases, so it was impossible to determine what actions may have been taken in these cases.

Consequently, they were also dropped from the analysis. Sixteen cases were repeat entries, 6 were miscoded cases (non-noise) and one was not dealt with as it was anonymous.

This left 109 cases receiving some form of intervention from Environmental Services. The case files were examined for all 109 cases, and every action taken was recorded, together with the actual time taken or (where this was not recorded) an 'average' time was assigned, based on estimates provided by Environmental Service staff. The number of visits made and ultimate outcomes were also recorded.

The various actions that are involved in processing a case that results in a prosecution for noise nuisance are set out in Table 8.1, together with the estimated average time taken.

Next, an hourly cost was calculated for each grade of staff including the appropriate provision for overhead costs which we obtained directly from Environmental Services.[6] By following cases through and 'building up' the costs in this way it is possible to calculate the costs involved in each case according to the degree of involvement by Environmental Services and also the ultimate outcome.

The average cost per case according to this method of calculation was £12.06, which is considerably lower than the sum of £54.99 which was obtained as a result of the time monitoring exercise.

Figure 8.2: Break-down of noise complaints by category.

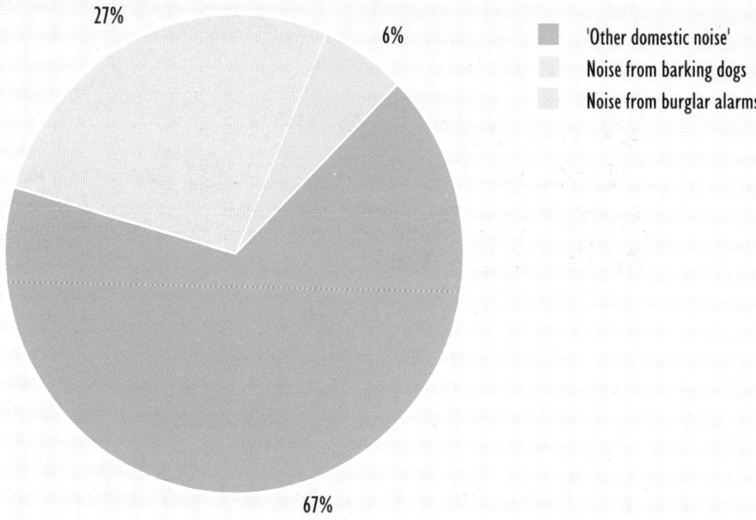

Source of data: Mediation research project case study based on Council A's Environmental Services Department

Table 8.1: Estimated average times required to process a case from initial complaint to prosecution for noise nuisance

Event/action	Average time	Comment
process DN1	15 mins	involves admin staff & includes receipt of complaint, processing & posting
assessment of log	30 mins	all other actions involve EHO/technician
site visit to investigate complaint (includes travel)	90 mins	
installation of remote monitoring equipment & analysis of results	150 mins	
visit and interview complainant & other witnesses	120 mins	Involves taking of formal statements prior to serving of notice, in case of appeal
preparation of abatement notice	60 mins	service is by post
repeat investigation phase	360 mins	to determine whether there has been a breach of the notice (is nuisance continuing at time of notice?)
decision on further enforcement measures /court proceedings	120 mins	
case preparation	240 mins	includes preparation of witness statements etc. and consultation with City solicitors
Total time (approx)	1185 mins	Approx 19.75 hours

As we have explained, however, the case analysis method is likely to yield a very conservative estimate of the total costs since it seems unlikely that every action will be accounted for, and no provision is made for general office time. Nevertheless, this approach does enable the relative costs to be calculated according to the level of intervention by Environmental Services and the outcome obtained. These are shown in Table 8.2.

It can be seen that the reason for the relatively low average total cost per case is that almost nine out of every ten complaints resulted in no action at all being taken by the department beyond the sending of a standard letter. In most cases this was because DN1 forms were sent out and not returned, though cynics might feel that this is a typical bureau-cratic response designed to limit the need for further intervention by the department.[7] If the 'DN1 only' cases are discounted the average cost per case is £81.71.

Most of the remaining cases (8.5%) are dropped for various reasons or referred elsewhere (1%). Where cases are referred elsewhere the cost to Environmental Services is relatively small, though additional costs will almost certainly be incurred by other departments or agencies. Unfortunately, it was not possible to quantify these. Similarly, additional costs are likely to be incurred[8] in respect of the small number of tenants who are rehoused or moved as a result of the complaint. In 3% of cases the complaints are investigated but the matter is dropped because no nuisance is found. Here the average cost is £98.

Formal legal remedies were pursued very rarely by Council A, though where abatement notices were served or the tenant was taken to court, the cost to environmental health services was very much higher, quite apart from any legal and admin costs that might be incurred.

We conclude this chapter with two case histories involving cases which were prosecuted for noise nuisance between 1 April 1994 and 31 March 1995. As in the case of the housing cases that resulted in court action, we have also been able to obtain details of the costs charged by Council A's administration and legal department which enable a 'cradle to grave' cost to be calculated.

It will be noted that in neither case did the legal proceedings appear to have curbed the nuisance complained of. Both cases, on the case of it, would

Table 8.2: Costs of intervention by Environmental Health according to form and level of intervention

Output label	Frequency	Percent	Average cost
No intervention by department	636	87.0	£3.34
Dropped, no further contact	38	5.0	£43.97
Alleged perpetrator rehoused or moved	3	0.25	£32.06
Referred to housing	4	0.5	£39.37
Dropped, nothing further can do	4	0.5	£41.43
Referred elsewhere	4	0.5	£42.63
Complainant rehoused	4	0.5	£64.43
Resolved following action by dept	12	1.5	£68.57
Dropped, no nuisance found	20	3.0	£98.27
Abatement notice served	3	0.5	£107.69
Prosecution	4	0.25	£267.45
Overall average	732	100	£12.06

Source of data: Mediation research project case study based on Council A's Environmental Services Department

appear to have been mediatable, though of course there can be no guarantee that mediation would have succeeded where the formal intervention undertaken by Environmental Health and the courts did not.

Case history 25

In the first case, a family living in a semi-detached house complained about the noise emanating from the adjoining house. This was occupied by a mother and her two teenage children. The main complaint related to the noise made by the son. It took the form of amplified music and loud television at unsociable hours. Environmental services' involvement in the case (including time input) is outlined in the table below.

Date	Action	Time estimate (mins)
26/2/92	Received complaint and sent information pack	2
9/5/94	Further complaint received	1
19/5/94	Complaint received via local councillor and replied to	20
12/10/94	Visit complainant	70
19/10/94	Obtain statement from complainant	60
25/10/94	Two officers interview alleged perpetrators	120*
2/11/94	Abatement notice types and served	30
14/11/94	Further complaint received	10
22/11/94	Interview complainant	50
5/12/94	Phone calls to complainant and alleged perpetrator	30
14/12/94	Two officers interview alleged perpetrator	100*
16/12/94	Enquiry from the complainant	10
20/12/94	Typing and drafting letters	45
23/12/94	Telephone call to the complainant	10
2/2/95	Further statement taken from the complainant	60
9/2/95	Letter to alleged perpetrator	30
9/2/95	Letter to Chief Constable	20
16/2/95	Two officers visit alleged perpetrator	120
6/3/95	Consider letter from social services	10
28/3/95	Further complaint from local councillor	10
8/3/95	Consider police officer's statement	30
10/4/95	Consider further noise incident data	10
2/6/95	Consider further data and updated statements	15
12/6/95	Consider other police officer's statements	15
	Compilation of prosecution file by environmental health officer	180
	Liaison with admin. and legal	60
	Total time taken	1218

* total time for both officers taken together.
The visits in the table above include travel time.

The case was heard in the magistrates court in February 96. The defendant was found guilty. He was given a conditional discharge and was bound over for twelve months. No fine was imposed, but the defendant was ordered to pay seventy pounds towards the council's costs.

In the short period which had elapsed between the court hearing and the writing of this report a complaint was made that the defendant had played loud music again. The complainants were advised to keep a log of any further disruption.

The total time expended by Environmental Health officers until June 1996 came to over 20 hours, at a total cost of £392.92. The cost of the involvement by the administration and legal department was assessed at £567.00,[9] making a grand total of £959.92.

Case history 26

The second case is an extremely lengthy one, which has spanned a number of years. Initially, the family who are now the subject of the complaint complained about building work in an adjacent property. The complaint was not upheld because building work, provided it is conducted during reasonable hours over a reasonable time period, does not constitute a statutory nuisance. The family who made the complaint allegedly started to retaliate by hammering on the adjoining wall. This is alleged to have continued even after the occupants who had carried out the building work had sold the property and it had become occupied by another family with an adult child. The new occupants made a number of complaints about the noise and finally environmental services decided to prosecute. The table below outlines the actions of environmental services from the point when the case came live.

Action	Time estimate (mins)
Visit complainant	120
Phone call to social worker	10
Phone call to complainant	30
Visit alleged perpetrators together with a principal social worker	120*
Visit complainant	60
Visit alleged perpetrator together with a principal social worker	120*
Phone call to complainants	10

Case conference involving principal environmental health officer, general practitioner, principal social worker, solicitor and consultant psychiatrist	120*
Phone call to complainant	10
Phone call to complainant	10
Preparing letters and notices	60
Serving notices	60
Phone call to complainant	10
Case conference involving principal environmental health officer, a social worker and a general practitioner	120*
Phone call to complainant	10
Going through logs and documents	60
Visit to complainant to take statements	90
Meeting with solicitor	30
Visit complainant to take statements	75
Serving summons	5
Putting file together and liaison with solicitors	600
Total time taken by Environmental Services	1730

* The times indicated are for the environmental health officer only. The visits and the serving of the summons do not in this case include travel time but serving of notices does.

The defendants were the parents in the household (they have an adult son). They were each fined thirty pounds following a guilty plea, and there was no application for costs.

This case took up a total of over 29 hours, and we calculate the cost to the Environmental Services department alone as being £674.39. The cost to the administration and legal department was assessed at £362.50 making a combined cost of £1036.89. As can be seen, there were also substantial additional costs to other departments and agencies.

The problem has recurred since the hearing and has become live again as far as environmental services are concerned. Instructions were given to recommence proceedings on 12 August 1996, and the case first came to court again on 1 October 1996. Neither the outcome nor the costs involved in the new proceedings were known at the time of writing.

Notes

1 There were 846 complaints about noise out of a total of 2752 complaints relating to noise, refuse, smoke and other matters.

2 Exceptions are made in cases involving elderly, infirm or disabled complainants, however.

3 Complaints about noise from burglar alarms may not necessarily entail the same costs as other domestic noise cases, and most of these probably do not involve neighbour disputes.

4 Of these, 32 involved complaints about burglar alarms and 10 were categorised as 'other domestic noise'.

5 Where a DN1 is returned by a complainant, the case is supposed to retain its original job-number in order to ensure that complaints are not 'double-counted'. There were records of 525 DN1 forms having been sent, together with a further 98 cases which were opened and closed in the same day, for which there is no record of any action having been taken. Environmental Service staff explained that these cases were also likely to have resulted in a DN1 being sent, but no further action on the part of the department.

6 See Appendix 4 for details of how these costs were calculated.

7 In twelve of the cases a DN1 was returned but the matter was resolved without further intervention by the department.

8 As we saw in Chapter 6 (page 57ff above), the cost to the Housing Department in such cases can be considerable.

9 This assumes an hourly rate of £50.00 per hour.

Comparing the costs and effectiveness of mediation and conventional responses to neighbour disputes

Introduction: outlining our approach

We have already made the point in our opening chapter that undertaking any form of conventional cost effectiveness analysis in the public sector cannot be an exact science, since the methodological problems it involves are compounded by the even more acute difficulties relating to the availability and reliability of the data that it requires. Moreover, seeking to compare mediation with conventional responses to neighbour disputes raises two sets of additional problems.

The first is that neighbour dispute mediation is at present largely conducted within the voluntary sector.[1] Moreover, as we have seen, most community mediation services rely heavily, and many exclusively, on the commitment of trained but volunteer mediators in order to provide the service. Comparing mediation with local authority responses to neighbour disputes thus involves a cross-sectoral comparison between public and voluntary sectors, which raises additional methodological problems of its own. The main difficulty here involves the largely technical problem of how to establish a 'level playing field', particularly in relation to cost-based comparisons; though it also raises policy issues to do with future funding arrangements and the potential for expanding the scope of mediation.

A second, and more fundamental methodological problem stems from the fact that on a range of other issues also, the differences between mediation and local authority responses to neighbour disputes are so acute that 'like' is not being compared with 'like' in any meaningful sense. These differences have also to be taken into account in any attempt to compare the costs and effectiveness of the contrasting approaches.

Our approach in this chapter involves a combination of the quantitative techniques that are associated with conventional forms of cost benefit analysis with a more qualitative assessment of the additional factors that also need to be addressed before any overall conclusions can be reached.

Our first task has been to devise a method of accurately assessing and calculating the 'resource costs' that are involved in the mediation of neighbour disputes by community mediation services. Then we consider the extent to which it is possible – within the constraints imposed by the methodological and data availability problems to which we have referred – to undertake a similar exercise in relation to the alternative processes deployed by local authority housing and environmental services departments.

The next step involves an attempt to compare the benefits associated with the two sets of processes in terms of their 'outputs' and also the quality of their outcomes – again within the limits imposed by the currently available data. Here the need for a more qualitative approach quickly becomes apparent.

Based on this analysis, we offer in the final section our own assessment of the cost effectiveness of mediation in comparison with more traditional ways of dealing with neighbour disputes.

Calculating the resource costs for mediation services

This part of the study is principally based on a very detailed analysis of the relevant case record and financial data for three highly contrasting community mediation services. Between them they provide examples of the three main types of service currently in existence.

Sandwell Mediation Service is a well-established and relatively well-funded service,[2] and is somewhat unusual in relying principally on professional mediators rather than volunteers. It also had the additional advantage, from our point of view, of maintaining exceptionally detailed and comprehensive case records, which enabled us to develop and refine our approach.

Derby Mediation Service also maintains very detailed records, but is a more recently established medium volume service that relies very heavily on volunteer mediators. In this latter respect at least it is perhaps representative of the great majority of community mediation services currently in existence.

Finally,[3] Bolton Neighbour Dispute Service is unique in being the sole example of an alternative 'in-house' model for the delivery of mediation services since it is funded by and operates from within Bolton Metro's housing department, though it maintains, and is keen to emphasise, its independence of the council in terms of its policy and approach.

For each service we sought the following information:

- up-to-date case statistics including data relating to selected outcomes;

- income and expenditure accounts relating to the period for which statistics were requested;[4]

- an estimate of the proportion of time devoted directly to neighbour mediation work by each of the grades of people working for the service;

- an estimate of the average time taken to perform each of the main 'process activities' that might be involved in a typical mediation case;

- a small number of case histories to illustrate the benefits of mediation and, if possible, the less easily quantifiable human costs incurred as a result of neighbour disputes.

In the case of Sandwell we undertook a far more intensive analysis which involved the abstraction of all relevant input and output data from every neighbour dispute case file relating to the first six months of 1995.[5] In addition, the staff at Sandwell agreed to take part in a time-monitoring exercise for a four week period ending the 15th October 1995,

which we used both in order to obtain more reliable information about the proportion of time devoted to neighbour-dispute mediation, and also as a means of cross-checking the reliability of the time allocation estimates we requested from them.[6]

With the aid of this data we were able to quantify the time taken to complete virtually every action involved in processing a case from start to finish. Where this was not possible for a particular event, we substituted the average value derived from those cases where the information was available, and recalculated the data on this basis.

Our analysis suggested that, on average, the length of time expended on each case was 10.37 hours (see Table 9.1).[7] We then apportioned these hours between each of the three main grades of staff at Sandwell.[8] The next step was to apply the information we obtained from the time monitoring exercise to exclude time spent on 'non core activities' such as victim offender mediation, victim support work, consultancy work and certain other non case-specific administrative tasks such as fundraising and PR work. All time spent on case-specific administrative work including training, case management etc. was included in the calculations.

We were then able to calculate the salary and add-on costs for each grade of staff in relation to the service as a whole, and also in relation to the two main types of mediation offered. As can be seen from Table 9.1, the total average cost per case for neighbour dispute mediation at Sandwell was £251.86.[9]

Using this approach, we were also able to calculate how many additional cases it might be possible for Sandwell Mediation Service to take on if its funding arrangements were sufficiently secure to obviate the need to spend time on 'indirect' activities including fund-raising, PR, consultancy and victim support work.[10] This would make it possible to increase the capacity of the service from the then-current level of 137 to 236, the effect of which would be to reduce the average cost per case to £191.88.

Table 9.1: Costings for Sandwell Mediation Service based on time sheet data

Caseload	137
Av. hrs per case	10.37
Full costs per case	£251.86
'Net cost' per case	£191.88

Table 9.2: Costings for Derby Mediation Service based on estimates and reported weekly working hours

Caseload	162
Av. hrs per case	8.8
Actual costs per case	£81.11
'Imputed cost' per case	£162.29

Although we did not have any time monitoring data for Derby, we were able to calculate average cost-per-case figures for this service also, based on estimates for the time taken to complete each case-related activity plus the reported weekly working hours. These figures are shown in Table 9.2. Since all the direct mediation work at Derby is undertaken by volunteer mediators, the actual cost per case is calculated by dividing the overall costs of the service by the hours spent on cases by the mediators. This produces an average of £81.11 per case. It is also possible to calculate what the average cost would be if mediators were paid for their services.[11] The effect would be to increase the average cost per case to £162.29.

Unfortunately, it was not possible to calculate the costs for Bolton Neighbour Dispute Service on the same basis, since we were unable to obtain details for the actual times spent by volunteer mediators for the period we were investigating. Consequently, it has only been possible to make a crude estimate of the average cost per case by dividing the total cost of the service by the number of cases that were dealt with in this period. Because the number of cases that were accepted by the service in 1994 was relatively small (82), this works out at an average cost per case of £428.82. Although we were unable to ascertain the actual time spent by volunteers, we did get the impression that those cases that are taken on by Bolton Neighbour Dispute Service may be dealt with more intensively than is the case for other community mediation services.

Calculating the resource costs in this way for mediation services is relatively straightforward provided the relevant information is fully recorded, and for two of our three case studies we are reasonably confident that the average costs we have identified are realistic, and represent the full actual costs to the service itself.[12]

As we have seen in the previous three chapters, it is much more difficult to calculate precisely the full range of resource costs that are incurred by local authority housing and environmental services[13]

Table 9.3: Cost of intervention by local authority housing departments according to form and level of intervention

Form of intervention	Estimated unit cost	
	Itemised Cost £	Total Cost £
Informal intervention over 12 mths by area housing officers only	50.00	
'Special tenancy transfer' involving one party to a dispute:		
Housing office staff costs	80.00	
Cost of special cases procedure for priority rehousing	141.44	
Lost rent, repairs, void protection etc.	602.41	
Total cost		823.85
Case involving legal advice stopping short of formal court action:		
Housing office staff costs	260.00	
Cost of legal advice provided by Admin and Legal Dept	104.77	
Total cost		364.77
Notice to Seek Possession served:		
Housing office staff costs	357.45	
Legal and Admin costs	238.53	
Total cost		595.98
Application for injunction:		
Housing office staff costs	339.00	
Legal and Admin costs	900.00	
Total cost		1239.00
Granting of (contested) possession order:		
Housing office staff costs	1296.25	
Legal and Admin costs	2611.40	
Total cost		3907.65

in relation to neighbour disputes. Nevertheless, in the next section we will bring together the various elements we have been able to calculate in an attempt to compare the costs of mediation with the cost of more conventional ways of dealing with neighbour disputes, and also to assess the scope for other potential savings to be made in cases for which mediation may prove suitable.

Comparing the cost of mediation and conventional ways of dealing with neighbour disputes on a 'unit cost' basis

We begin this section by bringing together and summarising the costs associated with various forms and levels of intervention on the part of local authority housing departments.[14] These costs have been calculated on the basis of the best available data[15] and are depicted in Table 9.3, though the figures need to be interpreted with great care in the light of the qualifying remarks that follow:

- Taking into account only the salary and related costs of housing department area staff, a very conservative estimate[16] is that an average of at least £50 is likely to be spent on every 'live' neighbour dispute case on which action is taken in the course of a year.

  It is very important to note, however, that this figure is likely to significantly understate the average cost per 'completed' neighbour dispute case since it only relates to the sum spent on 'live' neighbour dispute cases over a given twelve month period. It does not, therefore, take into account time and costs incurred in respect of those cases in which action was taken outside the monitoring period.[17]

  Neighbour dispute cases vary considerably in terms of the amount of staff time they consume. In our case study based on area office 'a' in Council A, housing officer costs over one year ranged from £7.04 to £276.16. Over the life of a dispute the sums involved can be considerably higher than this, however, and in at least six of our case histories we calculated that the total staff costs for the housing department alone were in excess of £450 (the maximum being £2,450). The more intensive the involvement by housing staff, the greater the potential scope for savings to be made in cases that can be successfully dealt with by means of mediation.

- As can be seen from Table 9.3, the cost of intervention is considerably greater in cases where the housing department's responds to a neighbour nuisance complaint by moving one of the parties. In cases such as these, we have calculated that the total direct housing office staff costs including the processing of the special cases application are likely to exceed £221.44 per case (also a conservative estimate). Once the indirect costs associated with lost revenue and increased expenditure on repairs, refurbishment and allocations are taken into account the average cost per case could be at least as high as £823.85 per case.

- Where neighbour disputes result in the threat or use of formal legal remedies, the overall costs are likely to be greater still. Based on our case study

of Council B's Legal and Admin records (see Chapter 8), it appears that in a case involving advice only, the additional costs could easily amount to an additional £100 or more per case. The cost to the housing department is also likely to be greater in such cases, and we estimate that the combined cost in a typical case could amount to over £350.

- Where a Notice to Seek Possession is sought, the legal costs are likely to be greater, and the involvement of housing officers is also frequently quite intensive in such cases. The combined figure we have given for housing and legal costs (£595.98) assumes that just a single notice is served; but very often if this fails to abate the nuisance a second or subsequent notices could be served, particularly if there are problems persuading witnesses to come to court. In one such case from Council B, involving two notices to seek possession,[18] the cost to the housing department was £430.12, while the legal costs amounted to £838.00, making a total of £1268.12.

- The cost of obtaining an injunction is likely to be between £800 and £1,000. The cost of housing office staff is likely to be variable according to the complexity and intractability of the case but could well bring the total to over £1,200.

- In the relatively few cases where possession proceedings are brought, the cost to the legal and administration department could easily exceed £2,500, and in a few particularly intractable cases[19] the cost to the housing department could be almost as great. In case 24, for example, the cost to housing was £2,419.42, while the legal costs were £2,713.70 (making a combined total of £5,133.12. Considerable as the combined costs are in cases such as this, the overall cost to the public purse is likely to be greater still where the proceedings are contested, as we explained in Chapter 8.

- Finally, one additional qualification that also needs to be emphasised is that the costs set out in Table 9.3 do not include any 'external costs' that might accrue to other council departments such as Environmental Health[20] and Social Services, or to agencies such as the police. Nor does it attempt to quantify the human, financial and social costs to the disputants themselves and others who may be affected by the dispute (including the personal and psychological effects that neighbour disputes might have on housing staff themselves).

As we explained in Chapter 6, however, housing departments are liable to incur other costs in relation to neighbour disputes quite apart from those associated with any intervention they may choose to make. For example, where neighbour nuisance results in property damage, the department may have to bear the cost of any repairs where these cannot be recovered from those responsible.

Some of this is likely to consist of damage to property that is sustained in the course of an identifiable dispute,[21] and in some of the case histories we examined, the damage appeared to be considerable. In Chapter 6 we estimated that in a single housing area,[22] the number of properties sustaining damage as a result of neighbour disputes or acts of neighbour nuisance (including vandalism) during 1995-6 was about 46, and the average repair cost per property was £68.22. In at least one of the other areas from which we drew our case histories, both the number of repairs and also the amount of damage involved was considerably greater than this.

Not all of these cases would be suitable for mediation. Indeed, in many cases the perpetrators of the damage might well be unknown. However, in cases that can be successfully resolved by means of mediation[23] there could also be an additional saving for the housing department besides those we have identified already, if this helps to avert further property damage.

Assessing the scope for savings as a result of increased use of mediation

The case for making greater use of mediation in the context of neighbour disputes is not founded on financial considerations so much as its claim to offer a potentially more constructive way of resolving a category of disputes that has not proved amenable to conventional forms of dispute resolution. However it would be unrealistic to suppose that the debate over its merits could be divorced entirely from considerations of cost. So how does mediation compare with conventional approaches in terms of its cost effectiveness?

First, as we have seen, mediation can be a very intensive process and is by no means a 'cost-free' option, even taking into account the fact that many services rely heavily on volunteers. On the face of it, even Derby's relatively low average cost per case of £81 may seem expensive compared with the average amount spent per case by housing and environmental service departments.

However, our findings suggest that the relatively low cost-per-case figures which we have calculated for housing and environmental service departments in particular, are largely a reflection of the fact that the great majority of neighbour dispute cases receive very limited attention from hard pressed public agencies. It is thus very important when comparing the different approaches to take into account the amount of input, and also its effectiveness, as well as the costs. These are issues that we will address in the next section. Meanwhile, it is also important to note that in many such cases other agencies such as social services and the police may also have been involved, so that the costs we have been seeking to establish are by no means the only ones incurred.

However, for the minority of cases that are dealt with more intensively the costs can be considerable, particularly where this involves legal intervention or a change of tenancy. Indeed, when compared with the costs incurred in some of the case histories we have been looking at, even the relatively high unit cost associated with a professional mediation service such as Sandwell's looks reasonably modest at around £250 on average, irrespective of any advantage it may have in resolving disputes more successfully. As we have seen, in principle it should be possible to reduce the costs to below £200 per case provided the service is able to run at 'full' capacity, though this assumes guaranteed funding.

For most 'routine' noise disputes our findings suggest that, purely on the basis of financial considerations, it would cost more to refer these to mediation than to deal with them by means of the current procedure; though in the great majority of cases in Council A, at least, this means that little or no action is taken to resolve the complaint. Compared with the cost of investigating an alleged statutory noise nuisance case however, at £98.27 it would be marginally cheaper to refer the matter to a voluntary mediation service of the kind operated by Derby

Mediation Service. For the minority of cases that result in formal legal intervention there would be a considerable cost advantage, as we have seen, if such cases could be dealt with by means of mediation, even on the basis of a paid service such as Sandwell's, and even discounting the additional legal costs involved.

When compared with the cost of informal intervention by housing officers the comparison is much less straightforward, given the different cost elements that need to be taken into consideration; and also the considerable variation in the level of involvement by housing officers even in cases where no formal action is taken. Here the 'base-line' figure appears to be an exenditure of £50 on average in direct and associated salary costs for every 'live' neighbour dispute case on which action is taken over a twelve month period. As we have seen, however, there is considerable variation in the amount of housing officer time devoted to such cases, which can also generate a variety of additional costs for the department.

There would appear to be scope for significant savings to be achieved in respect of some of the more intractable neighbour disputes – even those that are dealt with informally – if mediation could be successfully deployed in resolving them. Once again the cost advantage in favour of mediation (assuming it can deliver the goods and that such cases are suitable for referral) would appear to be overwhelming in cases that are currently dealt with by means of rehousing or the various legal sanctions that are available.

So far we have simply been comparing the costs of dealing with neighbour disputes without any reference to the benefits or quality of service that is provided. These are issues that we seek to address in the next section.

Comparing the merits of mediation and conventional responses to neighbour disputes

In comparing the quality of dispute processing methods, we suggest that it is important to differentiate between two very different measures of 'quality' or 'value added'. We refer to these as 'output measures' and 'outcome measures' respectively.

We would define 'output measures' as those steps that have been taken in order to resolve a dispute, irrespective of its outcome. They might include the number of cases accepted for intervention as well as the level and type of intervention deployed. Assessing the performance of different dispute resolution techniques in relation to output measures should involve both quantitative analysis – how much (or how little) is attempted? – and also qualitative analysis – how effective are the different forms of intervention likely to be?

'Outcome measures' are used to assess the quality of the end result, and here we will assess the extent to which mediation can be compared (whether quantitatively or qualitatively) with alternative forms of dispute resolution in the light of the available data, and what further investigation might be required beyond the scope of this study.

One of the most obvious 'output measures' consists of the number (or proportion) of disputes deemed eligible for assistance. On the face of it, mediation services compare very favourably with both environmental services and housing departments in terms of the range of neighbour disputes they may be willing to take on.

We have already made the point that their criteria for accepting cases are much less restrictive, in the sense that it is not necessary for the complainant to establish that there has been a breach of a tenancy condition or behaviour that is sufficiently serious as to constitute a 'statutory nuisance'. In other words, there is no 'threshold of seriousness' that needs to be satisfied before a case can be taken on for mediation. Consequently, around 75% of all referrals are accepted by community mediation services.

Probably the most restrictive stipulation imposed by most mediation services is the requirement that both parties (or at least the 'first party') should be willing to participate in the process, but since mediation depends for its success on parties being prepared to work for the resolution of their own disputes, rather than having a solution imposed on them this is at least a 'functional' requirement.

The potentially restrictive effects of a 'seriousness threshold' are demonstrated most vividly in respect of the 'attrition rate' we observed regarding the way complaints are dealt with by Council A's Environmental Service department (see Table 8.2 on page 72). The number of complaints that are taken up by the department is drastically reduced by obliging complainants to 'register' their complaint by using an officially prescribed form that requires a considerable effort to complete. Persistence also appears to be required thereafter since almost half of the remainder are dropped, either because there is no further contact, or it is concluded that nothing more can be done at the outset.

Fewer than 5% of the original complaints are investigated, and most of these are taken no further, having established that no statutory nuisance has been committed. Only a tiny proportion of complaints are prosecuted or result in one or other of the parties being moved.

Unfortunately, it is virtually impossible to establish what the 'attrition rate' might be for housing departments since, unlike environmental services, it appears that many complaints that are deemed to be trivial are simply not recorded. Of those that are recorded, it seems that housing officers are more likely than their colleagues in Environmental Services to investigate the complaint (see Table 3.5 on page 19), and in over two thirds of cases this will involve a visit to the complainant. The party being complained of is visited in nearly 60% of cases, and warning letters are sent out in approximately half of all cases. However, housing officers – like Environmental Health Officers – make little use of their formal legal powers.

The Area Manager for Council A's housing area 'a' explained that one of the main reasons for this is that only the most serious of cases, backed by the most compelling evidence, would justify the extreme measure of taking tenants to court and seeking possession of their house. In less serious cases, or where there is little corroborating evidence, there is usually little the Housing Department can do beyond warning the tenants.

Thus, although the involvement of housing services in neighbour disputes is often highly intensive, as we have seen, its effectiveness may be open to question. Much of the time seems to be spent collecting and assessing evidence of anti-social behaviour and relaying accusations and counter accusations.

One of the main problems is that the 'fault-based' nature of all the formal legal remedies encourages a quasi-legalistic approach to the problem even though the vast majority of disputes are never aired in court. Moreover, the very process of taking evidence and assessing its quality may inhibit the

adoption of a more constructive 'problem-solving' approach. This is particularly evident in the very common practice of issuing complainants with 'diary sheets', the effect of which may be to foster a more adversarial approach.

There is also the very real risk that in failing to convince complainants that it is taking effective action, the council may all too often find itself on the receiving end of complaints about its role in the dispute. We have come across a number of examples of this tendency in the case histories we have examined earlier in the report.

Finally, as we have seen, even when more formal methods of enforcement are adopted, it is by no means certain that these will resolve the problem giving rise to the complaint, in spite of the time and expense that is invariably involved.

On the face of it, mediation would appear to offer a more constructive way of dealing with at least some kinds of neighbour disputes, assuming that parties are willing to give it a try. Comparing the outcomes that are achieved by the two sets of processes is fraught with difficulty, however. Two major inter-related problems are, first, how to define success, and secondly how to measure it.

As far as public sector agencies are concerned there is a tendency to equate 'success' with non-recurrence of the complaint, and little attempt appears to be made to record or monitor the effect of their interventions. It is therefore difficult to measure the success of their interventions, partly because the data may not be available, but also because there may be some other explanation for a cessation of the complaints. For example, a complainant may have concluded that there is no point persisting in the complaint; or the person whose behaviour is being complained of may have left the area or may even have been arrested and tried for a criminal offence, as we discovered when examining one of the case histories we obtained from Council B.

Within mediation services, the outcome of any intervention is much more likely to be recorded,[24] and a few services do attempt to monitor this by seeking feed-back from the parties. However there is a lively debate within mediation as to whether success is best defined in terms of encouraging parties to reach an agreement, or whether the aim should be to 'transform' the hostile relationship between the parties by encouraging dialogue

Figure 9.1: Outcomes recorded for Council A housing department interventions (area 'a')

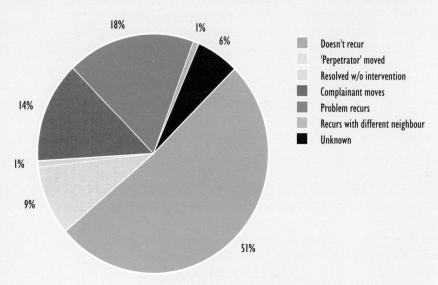

18%   1%
        6%

14%

1%

9%

51%

Doesn't recur
'Perpetrator' moved
Resolved w/o intervention
Complainant moves
Problem recurs
Recurs with different neighbour
Unknown

Source of data: Mediation research project case study based on Council A's Housing Services Department

between the parties irrespective of any agreement or behavioural changes that might result from this.

As part of our case study involving Council A's housing area office 'a', we attempted to record the outcomes reached in respect of all 117 cases we examined, and also to compare them in terms of their direct costs to the housing department.[25] The outcomes themselves are shown in Figure 9.1. The equivalent set of findings, which we obtained from our survey of Community Mediation Services, is shown on page 28 (see Figure 4.7).

Unfortunately, the categories used to record outcomes are quite different, so it is difficult to make direct comparisons; though to some extent this is inevitable given the differences between the two sets of processes. In support of mediation, it might be argued, firstly, that the proportion of disputes that are known to recur following some intervention by housing officers is more than twice as big as the proportion of mediation attempts that remain 'unresolved' because of irreconcilable differences between the parties. Secondly, the proportion of mediated disputes that results in some measure of agreement or reconciliation is somewhat higher (58%) than the proportion of 'housing' cases in which the complaint does not recur.

However, nearly one in three mediated cases are terminated for other reasons – usually because

one of the parties does not wish to proceed, and possibly these should also be counted as 'failures'. Conversely, just because a complaint does not recur does not mean that the problem has been resolved. The most effective way of comparing outcomes between the two sets of processes would be to undertake a comparative consumer satisfaction survey. Unfortunately, this lay beyond the scope of the current project, but is one of a number of suggestions for further research which we will summarise in the final chapter.

Meanwhile, we will conclude this chapter with three final case histories which were all dealt with by Sandwell Mediation Service. They provide a good illustration of the way mediation can be used to resolve at least some neighbour disputes of the kind that are routinely referred to local authority housing and environmental services. Each example includes the full costs incurred by the mediation service, which have been calculated on the same basis as for the larger sample we presented at the beginning of this chapter.[26]

Mediation case histories

There are several noteworthy features of all three cases. In the first place, it appears that in each case the matter was referred to the mediation service at a relatively early stage in the dispute, before attitudes had become too hardened. However, it is also worth noting that relations between the parties were nevertheless severely strained by the time the mediation service became involved, particularly in case histories 28 and 29. Secondly, other agencies had been involved in all three cases, and had tried unsuccessfully to resolve the problem. Most important of all, however, is the fact that in all three cases the parties were willing to participate in the mediation process and make a genuine attempt to find a solution to the problem. Moreover, support from other agencies also proved extremely constructive in all three cases.

The first of the cases is typical of a good many

neighbour disputes in that the main complaint was noise-related and had to do with the fact that the parties' lifestyles were not entirely compatible.

Case History 27

This dispute was between a young couple in their mid twenties with two young children and their neighbour, who was a recently widowed woman in her mid sixties and lived alone.

The young family complained of noise nuisance caused by their neighbour leaving her radio on whenever she was out of the house. This extended to leaving the radio on twenty four hours a day when she went to stay with relatives at the weekends. The young family found the noise disturbing, especially as one of their children had recently undergone surgery following a long and painful serious illness. The child's sleep and rest during the day and early evening were being disturbed by the constant noise from the radio.

The mother of the young family had approached her neighbour about the problem but no satisfactory solution had been reached. The family's social worker had also made an approach but this had not been fruitful. The social worker suggested mediation and contacted the local mediation service.

The social worker telephoned the mediation service in July 1995. They contacted the mother of the young family and arranged a home visit for the following day. The next day a letter was sent to the neighbour who phoned the mediation service and was visited the following week. There was one further visit to the young family, and finally a face-to-face mediation session in August.

In the face-to-face meeting, the mother was able to inform her neighbour about her son's illness and treatment and explain how the noise was affecting the family. The neighbour was able to explain that since she had become widowed she had a fear of entering a silent house and an even greater fear of finding her home had been burgled. She said that she left her radio on to give the impression that someone was at home and to prevent her having to enter a silent house. After listening to her neighbour and the problems of their child's illness she also accepted for the first time how her actions were affecting her neighbours. She said that her family had insisted that she had a burglar alarm installed

after the death of her husband but explained that she never used it for fear of it 'going off' while she was away from home.

In the meeting it was agreed that she would use the burglar alarm rather than leaving the radio on. It was also agreed that a contact number and whereabouts would be left with the mother of the young family if required. The family received a full apology from their neighbour for the distress she had caused and both parties left the meeting on good terms.

A month after the meeting the mediator received a 'Thank you card' from both parties. Follow-up contact six months after the meeting revealed that both parties were still enjoying a good relationship.

The case involved 4.83 hours of the mediators' time and was costed at £41.46.

The next case involved a serious inter personal dispute that had already resulted in an assault by one of the parties on the other, and threatened to escalate still further when the police, who had frequently been summoned to deal with the problem, referred the parties to the mediation service. An interesting feature of the case is the active participation of the local beat officer, both in initiating the referral and also during the course of the mediation process itself.

Case History 28

This dispute began with a problematic relationship between the children of two families. There was a history of name calling, threats and some physical contact between the children. This escalated to include the parents. As well as name calling and threats between the parents, there was an actual assault by the mother of one set of children upon the mother of the other family.

The police had been called as a result of the dispute on numerous occasions and were considering arresting both parties with a view to 'binding them over'. In addition, both parties had complained to their local neighbourhood housing office but had been advised that the Council could do nothing because one of the parties was an owner occupier. One party had also visited the local Citizen's Advice Bureaux, who had suggested involving a solicitor. The local beat officer suggested mediation and referred the disputants to the local mediation service.

The case was referred by the beat officer in April 1996. One of the parties telephoned the mediation service two days later and a home visit was arranged for the following week. Following this visit, a letter was sent to the second party and they received a home visit the week after. There were two further visits to each party. One visit to each party was made with the local beat officer. The discussions were finalised with a face-to-face mediation meeting which was held in August.

During initial discussions, both parties stated that 'things had got out of hand' and that because of other problems they were experiencing in their own lives they had reacted aggressively towards one another. In the face-to-face meeting that followed, agreements were reached as to future behaviour and how both sets of parents would manage their children's conflict. It was agreed that both parents would discuss the conflict with their children and would ask for a face-to-face meeting to be held with the children if they thought it was necessary. The two families left the meeting on good terms.

Follow-up telephone calls to both parties and the beat officer later in August and to both parties in September revealed that there had been no further incidents between the children and the relationship between the parents had also improved.

A total of 11.45 hours was spent on the case by the mediation service at a cost of £282.45.

The final case history is a good example of a multi-party dispute in which various agencies, including both the local housing department and the police, had been actively involved, but to no avail. Feelings were evidently running very high on both sides, and this was reflected in two articles in the local newspaper in March 1996. One of these spoke of an 18 month period of 'mob rule' which had terrified local residents, while the other reported complaints by parents that their children were being harassed by residents who were 'anti children', and whose remarks were giving the estate the reputation of a no-go area. Equally noteworthy is the imaginative approach to the problem which combined a multi-agency approach with support for a 'self-help' response from the community. In many ways this final example, together with the two previous ones, offer a model of good practice which may help to counter the widespread view that neighbour disputes are invariably 'no-win' scenarios.

Case History 29

This case was one involving problems within the community rather than a dispute between one resident and another. A number of residents on a housing estate complained about the severely anti-social behaviour of youths on the estate. They complained about vandalism, pelting of houses and residents with bricks, and abuse and threats to worshippers at a local church by youths aged between 11 and 16. Parents of youths on the estate, on the other hand, stated that the complaints came from a clique of residents who were anti-children. They claimed that their children were subjected to foul- mouthed abuse from these residents, who they claimed were narrow minded. They complained that their children could not even play football on the estate without receiving abuse. They wanted to campaign for a play area for the children.

The housing department and police had been called in to deal with the dispute and a one hundred name petition had been handed to a Councillor. The housing department had written to five residents asking them to exert greater control over their children. In these letters the tenants were warned that they were breaching their tenancy conditions and would be served with notices seeking possession of their properties if they did not take action.

In March 1996, the police and the housing department requested the assistance of the local mediation service. The mediators met with statutory agencies in April and interviewed most of the residents in the area to assess their concerns and problems. It was noted that the young people in the area were not present at these interviews. A meeting was held with the Community Safety Officer and Youth workers in order to devise a plan of action to make contact with the young people. Also in April, one of the mediators made enquiries to the local brewery and planning department with regard to waste land in the area and a site meeting was held with other agencies in order to agree a plan of action. Meanwhile, complaints about nuisance from youths were still being made to the police and Housing Department.

In May, one of the mediators met with the young people in the area and collected their concerns and problems. The young people formed a management committee to liaise with residents and agencies in order to improve the area. A face-to-face meeting between the young people and the residents was held in June. This was poorly attended by the residents but there were reports from the residents of improvements in the road.

Youth workers continued to work with the young people and any isolated problems were addressed by them. One resident, for example, reported to the Housing Office that the front of her house had been used as a target for throwing mud. This information was relayed to the youth workers and, to the resident's surprise, the young people responsible arrived on her doorstep, apologised, removed all the debris and cleaned the front of her house. Another resident reported to the police that the rear window of his van had been smashed. Because of problems in the past he blamed the local young people. The young people heard about this and three of them called at the resident's home but his wife was too frightened to open the door. The same three youths returned later that evening and informed her husband that the person responsible for breaking the van window was an individual who did not live on the street. The resident was extremely grateful and passed the information on to the police. A Community Safety Officer continued to work with residents with a view to holding a planning meeting.

In September, residents reported that although they had been dreading the summer holidays they were pleased to report that there had been no major problems. One resident, who had put her house up for sale because of the previous problems, had taken her house off the market as she was happy to stay in the road. There was a meeting with residents and other agencies at which the residents formed a group to plan for the future with young people. Both groups continue to be supported by youth workers and the Community Safety Officer.

Although the dispute had appeared to be intractable at the outset, the combined efforts of the mediation service, the participants, and all the other agencies involved seem to have resolved a difficult set of problems. Not surprisingly, given the intensive involvement on the part of the mediation service, the case proved to be both time-consuming and costly for them, since it consumed a total of 68.52 hours at a cost of £842.32. Nor should it be overlooked that other agencies were also involved, and their costs have not been included since we had no details of their precise involvement.

However, it seems indisputable that two agencies in particular – the local housing department and the police – benefited significantly as a result of the outcome. The housing department were spared the expense of evicting or moving several residents, and may benefit indirectly still further if the threat to the reputation and desirability of the estate is alleviated by the positive resolution of the dispute. Similarly the police, who had been called out to the estate no fewer than 200 times in the six month period leading up to the mediation, stood to benefit from the improved state of relations. Following the mediation they had been called to the estate on just two occasions. However, the biggest beneficiaries of all, of course, were the parties themselves.

Notes

1 But not exclusively. At least one neighbour dispute service, in Bolton, operates as a quasi-autonomous unit within the council's housing department. Other councils, such as Dudley, employ neighbourhood conciliation officers whose remit includes providing a neighbourhood mediation service (see Karn, 1993: 83-4).

2 In common with a number of other services offering neighbour dispute mediation, it is also involved to a somewhat lesser extent in victim offender mediation and victim support work. This dual role also needs to be taken into account when calculating the resource costs that are involved.

3 We did also investigate MESH, which is based in Sheffield, as an example of a very recently established service, following its relaunch in 1995 on the strength of a much more secure funding base. However, we have not included this in the present analysis.

4 In most cases this was for 1994, but in the case of Sandwell we decided to focus on cases referred during a six month period between January and June 1995, for reasons described below.

5 A new recording system was introduced at the end of 1994, and greatly increased the quality and reliability of the case records, which is why we decided to look at the later period.

6 It was also important to try to establish the reliability of this approach in connection with the other case studies, for which we would not have the time-monitoring data.

7 This is very close to the average time obtained by applying the average times which staff at Sandwell estimated would be required to complete each of the case-specific event tasks, which worked out at 10.8 hours. This strengthened our confidence in the reliability of this technique for calculating case specific time values for our other case study areas, where it formed the basis of our calculations in the absence of any time monitoring information.

8 Project co-ordinator, administrator and mediator(s).

9 Inclusive of 'add-on' costs. The salary-only cost averaged out at £187.00. The detailed calculations from which these figures are derived can be seen in Appendix 5a–e.

10 There is scope for argument over the merits of excluding what might be termed administrative support costs in relation to community mediation services. When seeking to compare the net costs of mediation with alternative processes that do not have to expend part of their energies on such activities, the effect of including these elements might be thought to disadvantage those services operating in the voluntary sector. Moreover, if the funding arrangements for mediation services were to change in the future there might conceivably be less need to devote so much time and energy to these activities, which would enable more cases to be taken on each year. Nevertheless, under present funding arrangements these indirect activ-

ities are essential in order to maintain the service in operation. Since we are seeking to include all the relevant on-costs in respect of housing and environmental services, we have decided to include these on-costs for mediation also, in the interests of establishing a 'level playing field'.

11 Assuming an hourly rate of £7.38 per hour (April 1993 New Earnings survey). See Appendix 6 for detailed calculations relating to Derby Mediation Service.

12 However, they do not include whatever 'external' costs might be borne by the client and other agencies before the case is referred for mediation.

13 We have already considered some of the problems involved in relation to Environmental Services in Chapter 8 above.

14 See Table 8.2 above, for comparable figures for Environmental Health Services.

15 Where possible, we have relied on the results of our Council A case studies. However, in the case of disputes involving some form of legal intervention, our figures are based on actual examples obtained from Council B. They are probably best regarded as 'typical' costs, but it is difficult to know how representative they are since such cases are relatively infrequent and the issues raised and level of complexity can be very variable.

16 Since it is based on case-specific activities only (which may not always be fully recorded) and excludes time spent on non case-specific activities and general office time that could legitimately be apportioned to neighbour nuisance cases.

17 For cases just starting towards the end of the monitoring period or those substantially concluded by the time it began, the additional costs involved could be considerable and their inclusion would have tended to increase the average expenditure per case. Unfortunately it has not been possible to make any allowance for this because of limitations in the data that was available.

18 Not featured among our case histories.

19 For example, case history 24.

20 But see Table 8.2 which sets out the cost of various forms of intervention in respect of the Environmental Service department in Council A.

21 See, for example case histories 5, 6, 12, 17, 19 and 23.

22 Area 'a' in Council A.

23 See case history 29, below, for an example of the kind of case in which mediation might be able to resolve community disputes featuring acts of vandalism.

24 Though until recently recording practices have been very variable, which has greatly limited the comparability of the data that is available.

25 See Appendix 2b, Council A Area 'a' Table 6 for details.

26 And using the same approach as we used to assess the cost of intervention by public agencies such as housing and environmental services.

Policy implications and suggestions for further research

In the course of our report we have identified a number of policy issues that would appear to merit further consideration. We will deal with these under the following headings before setting out some suggestions for further research:

- Targeting the use of mediation

- Extending the use of mediation

- Promoting the greater use of mediation

Targeting cases for mediation

If there is one clear message to come out of the present research it is that neighbour disputes are infinitely variable in the form they take, their intensity and also their social and financial consequences. It would be unreasonable to expect any one approach to be capable of resolving all such disputes, and mediation is no exception. Indeed, we have deliberately included among our case histories examples of some of the more intractable neighbour disputes for which mediation would not seem to be the most appropriate response. There are also likely to be disputes for which mediation could potentially offer an effective solution, but not necessarily the cheapest one.

One important policy issue this raises is whether it is possible to articulate more clearly than at present (at either national or local level) the kind of disputes for which mediation might be considered an appropriate response, and to communicate this to potential referral agencies. This would have the advantage of concentrating the relatively expensive (and currently scarce) resource of mediation (even where volunteers are used) on those cases where the prospects of success are greatest, while avoiding inappropriate and potentially time consuming referrals that might most effectively be dealt with in other ways.

We have no easy answers to the question we have posed, but we do have a suggestion to make. In the light of the case histories we have assembled, we believe it might be possible to construct a typology of disputes, some of which would appear to lend themselves more readily to mediation than others. We offer this in the hope that it, or something like it, might be helpful in establishing a set of criteria for use by referral agencies and mediation services alike.

Despite their variability, we believe that the majority of neighbour disputes could be categorised under one of the following headings:[1]

- Disputes resulting from inconsiderate or mildly anti-social behaviour on the part of one or both (all) of the parties (see case histories 3, 8, 11, 20, 21 and 25);

- Disputes involving a more serious personality or life-style clash (see case histories 1, 2, 4, 8, 9, 10, 11, 12, 13, 14, 24 and 26);

- Disputes involving a degree of harassment and/or minor criminal acts relating to the dispute itself (see case history 15);

- Disputes where the neighbour nuisance element is an incidental by-product of some other activity or problem; e.g. disturbance resulting from domestic violence; drug use etc. (see case histories 7, 12, 17, 18, 22 and 23);

- Disputes involving serious harassment (including racial harassment), or where one of the parties is involved in serious criminal activity (see case histories 16, and possibly also case 13);

- Disputes involving 'care in the community' cases, or those in which one of the parties appears to have mental health problems (see case histories 5, 6 and 19).

LIVERPOOL
JOHN MOORES UNIVERSITY
AVRIL ROBARTS LRC
TITHEBARN STREET
LIVERPOOL L2 2ER
TEL. 0151 231 4022

Disputes resulting from inconsiderate or mildly anti-social behaviour on the part of one or both (all) of the parties

Although we have no means of knowing for certain,[2] we feel sure that this is probably the most numerous category of all, and may well account for a majority of those referred to both housing and environmental health officers, including most of those in which noise is an issue. Of the three housing managers with whom we discussed the proposed typology, two confirmed that this was indeed the case. In Council A's area 'a' 60% of disputes were said to fall into this category, while in area 'x' it was 70%. In Council B, only 39% of cases were felt to involve mildly anti-social behaviour (including complaints directed at children and young people).

These are the disputes that are likely to be least well served by current procedures since only in the most serious cases are they likely to constitute grounds for invoking the council's formal legal powers.

On the face of it, mediation appears to offer much the most effective way of dealing with the problem (except in those cases where a 'warning letter' or visit from the appropriate council officer is itself sufficient to resolve the matter).

The difficulty, from a purely financial cost-benefit point of view, is that the scope for savings in relation to such cases is very limited since, as we have seen, little or no action is likely to be taken in most cases by any of the existing agencies (particularly on the environmental health side). Indeed, mediation is likely to involve substantial additional costs in such cases when compared with current procedures. Because of the numbers involved, mediation services would probably find it difficult to cope with the demand if all such cases were to be referred, and this could seriously restrict their ability to take on more serious cases where the scope for savings (whether measured in financial, human or social terms) could be very much greater.

On the other hand, some disputes that start off as minor acts of incivility may degenerate into much more serious forms of hostility if effective action is not taken at a sufficiently early stage to defuse the issues and resolve the growing conflict between the parties. Case history 11 is probably a classic example of a series of minor acts of mildly inconsiderate behaviour escalating into something

much more serious, and the same probably also applies to a number of cases with even more tragic consequences, such as case history 3.

Disputes involving a more serious personality or life-style clash

These can be among the most difficult disputes to resolve for hard-pressed housing[3] and environmental health officers, and here mediation would appear to offer the most suitable approach and also the greatest scope for savings to be achieved. In Council A, our respondents indicated that approximately 10% of their neighbour disputes could be assigned to this category. In Council B the proportion was 20%.

However, if mediation is to succeed in such cases it is vitally important for it to be given a chance to work before attitudes begin to harden. The onus here is on the relevant council officers to be able to identify cases where, upon investigation, the existing noise nuisance controls are found to be inapplicable, and to make the referral. It should be noted that in many cases the issuing of diary sheets is unhelpful, in that it probably conveys an expectation of ultimate legal action, leading to the complainant actively listening out for the noise and possibly developing a more adversarial approach to the problem. Such cases also raise important policy issues relating to the willingness of officials and disputants to make use of mediation, and we will be returning to these later in the chapter.

For mediation services, the issue is one of managing resources (time, volunteers) in such a way as to be able to identify particularly pressing cases and, if necessary, to respond immediately to them. Where they are unable to do this (for example because of heavy case-loads), it could run the risk of discouraging future referrals.

More generally, it is in respect of cases such as these that conventional legal remedies are likely to be least effective, as we saw from a number of the case histories. There is now a growing recognition that adjudication may not be the most appropriate way to resolve such issues (Woolf, 1995) and there may well be a case for extending the legal aid scheme to cover alternative forms of dispute resolution such as mediation in such circumstances,[4] taking into account the availability of local mediation services and the parties' willingness to avail themselves of it when assessing the most appropriate forum in which to try and resolve the issues.[5]

Disputes involving a degree of harassment and/or minor criminal acts relating to the dispute itself

The feedback we received from our case study areas suggests that approximately 10% of neighbour disputes may fall into this category. Some mediation services themselves are reluctant to take on cases involving racial or any other forms of harassment, and some housing officers indicated in our questionnaire survey that they would be unwilling to refer these or cases involving criminal acts. While in such cases it is, of course, for the police to decide in the first instance whether formal action is required, we do not believe that mediation is intrinsically unsuitable for problems such as these, though much may depend on the particular circumstances of the case and also the skills and experience of the mediators concerned.

A number of mediation services are involved in victim/offender mediation as well as neighbour disputes, and at least where the criminal acts (minor assaults, criminal damage etc.) are incidental to the dispute, it may be more appropriate for them to be dealt with in this context rather than leaving all such matters to the police. Very often, either they or the Crown Prosecution Service may decide that it is not in the public interest to prosecute or issue a caution, in which case unless the case is referred for mediation the issues giving rise to the dispute may not be effectively addressed at all.

In fact, as we have seen, the police are already well represented on the steering committees of most community mediation services, and are themselves only too well aware of the limitations of conventional responses to neighbour disputes. In several of our case histories the suggestion to refer the matter to mediation came from the police. One example of good practice we encountered at Sandwell Community Mediation Service was to involve the local community constables in the mediation process in cases where the police had been called on to intervene in a dispute, informing them of any agreement reached between the parties.

Disputes where the neighbour nuisance element is an incidental by-product of some other activity or problem; e.g. disturbance resulting from domestic violence; drug use etc.

We came across a number of examples of such cases when compiling our case histories. Those we spoke to in our case study areas suggest that cases of this kind account for between 8 and 18% of the total caseload. Where the alleged perpetrator is as much of a victim as those making the complaints, the primary need is to resolve the main cause of the problem, and if mediation does have a role in such cases it is likely to be a subordinate one.

Case history 23, for example, provides one example of the role mediation might play in such a case. Here the nuisance was mainly being caused by the tenant's violent partners, and she was then being threatened (wrongly) for abusing her child. Assuming that those who were mainly responsible for the nuisance and abuse could be effectively dealt with by the police and courts it is possible to imagine mediation having a part to play in repairing relations between the tenant and her neighbours.[6]

Disputes involving serious harassment (including racial harassment), or where one of the parties is involved in serious criminal activity

Cases such as these can prove extremely time consuming for housing officers but are unlikely to be referred for mediation. Indeed, we imagine that many mediation services would themselves be reluctant to take on such cases.[7] They are in any event likely to be relatively infrequent and, according to our case study respondents, only account for 4-5% of their total caseload.

Disputes involving 'care in the community' cases

Finally, we came across a number of cases involving housing allocations under the 'care in the community' scheme, or those in which one (or more) of the parties appeared to have mental health problems. These were among the most distressing and intractable of all the disputes we came across. The human, social and economic costs that were incurred as a result of such disputes were among the highest of any of the categories we have been looking at, and virtually all the agencies involved (including many of the mediation services we spoke to) seemed at a loss when dealing with them.

The number of 'care in the community' cases that we came across was surprisingly large, and we were told that the problem was a growing one. Estimates provided by our case study respondents ranged between 4% and 10% of their total caseload. We suspect that only by improving the level of support provided, including the availability of sheltered accommodation where appropriate, could the problem be tackled, though we would be the first to acknowledge that the issues raised by such cases go far beyond those we were asked to address.[8]

In the light of the above analysis, we suggest that two key policy question need to be addressed. First, how to ensure that cases which might be suitable for mediation are referred at the most appropriate time; and secondly, whether there might now, or in the future (if demand were to escalate), be a case for 'targeting' the cases referred to or taken on by mediation services on the basis of their perceived seriousness.

One suggestion would be for agencies to develop a 'referral threshold' that would seek to strike a balance between not referring cases unnecessarily, while still ensuring that referrals to mediation are not made too late in the day for them to be effective. We are aware that slightly different considerations may apply in respect of housing and environmental service departments because of the nature and demands of their specific legal responsibilities. The proposal that follows is directed in the first instance at those whose involvement in neighbour disputes stems from their responsibilities as social landlords.

With regard to housing services, we would propose a flexible three-step response strategy as follows:

- step 1: in 'routine' cases issue the complainant with a 'self-help' pack[9] encouraging him/her to raise the matter directly with the other party and advising on how best to do this;[10] one important aim of the pack would be to reduce unrealistic expectations about the extent and effectiveness of existing legal powers and remedies;

- step 2: visit both parties if the complaints persist, and consider referring appropriate cases to mediation at that stage – i.e. *before* any diary sheets are issued (where used) or warning letters are sent. This is important, as the conventional response to neighbour disputes appears to encourage an adversarial approach that may often limit the prospects for successful mediation at a later stage. Our case study respondents informed us that the type of categories we propose would be workable, though there is obviously some overlap between them. Most felt that the majority of cases could be assigned to one or other of the categories at least after visiting one or both parties.[11] This is important as it suggests that it should be possible in most cases to make a decision on whether a case falls into a category that is suitable for referral for mediation without having to conduct a detailed (and expensive) investigation.

- step 3: if there is evidence that informal responses have been attempted without success, then consider whether the allegations are serious enough to warrant the use of formal measures. Only if this is the case should diary sheets[12] be issued and other measures contemplated (such as the use of professional witnesses etc.).

As far as Environmental Health Services are concerned, they have a legal duty to investigate a complaint, and to consider whether there is evidence of a statutory nuisance. We have become aware in the course of the research that services frequently discharge this duty by issuing 'diary sheets' as the first step in the investigation process. We have commented elsewhere that we do not think this approach is helpful since it runs the risk of locking complainants into an adversarial stance which may not be conducive to a satisfactory resolution of the complaints; and indeed may engender unrealistic expectations as to any formal action that might be taken by the council. We would therefore favour the adoption of a less confrontational approach which we believe would enhance the prospects of mediation being acceptable to both parties, and would therefore contribute to a successful outcome to the dispute.

Nevertheless, even where diary sheets are used, we believe there may be merit in adopting a 'twin-track' approach whereby complainants would be issued with the self-help pack at the same time as the diary sheets. There would be then be a need for the advantages and disadvantages associated with each approach to be spelt out in a covering letter.

At the same time, it may be worth considering at a national level whether more effective *preventive* measures could be taken, for example by adopting more stringent standards for the sound-proofing of new or refurbished multiple-occupation premises or for buildings that are being converted for multi-occupation. In principle it ought to be possible to investigate the costs and benefits of such an approach at relatively little expense.

This leads on to a further important point about any complaints system: all complaints should be recorded in such a way that (locally) common ones can be identified and lead to consideration of preventive measures. We make this recommendation not in order to make life easier for ourselves or fellow researchers but in order to facilitate the process of 'organisational learning'. This would pay dividends both at the local level, in developing more appropriate responses to pressing problems, and also at national policy-making level.

Extending the use of mediation

Given the ineffectiveness of existing approaches to many problems involving disputes between neighbours, we believe that there is a case for extending the use of mediation, particularly if ways can be found of 'targeting' it on those cases where the prospects for success (and the scope for significant reductions in the human, social and financial costs involved) are greatest. Nevertheless, this raises the important policy issue of how best to achieve this goal.

One obvious prerequisite is an increase in the number of community mediation services. There has been a dramatic expansion in recent years but, as we explained in chapter 4, many services are experiencing problems over funding, and the need to be constantly seeking new or maintaining existing sources of income can reduce the capacity of even established and relatively affluent services such as the one in Sandwell.

Our survey of community mediation services showed a clear correlation between the number of cases taken on and the total funds available to a service. All but one of the services receiving in excess of 150 referrals each year had funding in excess of £20,000 per annum. Thus, the most effective way of extending the use of mediation would be to find secure reliable sources of funding for new and existing services.

Currently the three main providers of funding[13] for mediation services are local government (which contributes 42% of current funding), followed by central government (23% if Safer Cities money is included) and national charities (which account for 17% of total funding).

The two main models for future funding arrangements would appear to be the 'victim support' model, whereby funding[14] is mostly used to pay for local co-ordinators to recruit, train and organise volunteers who provide the service; and the use of 'service contracts' between individual mediation services and local authority housing and environmental health departments.

The latter model has the advantage of gearing the level of funding (at least to some extent) to the number of cases dealt; and could in theory be used to provide payments for mediators on either a sessional or salaried basis. However, there are concerns with this model that the service might find itself restricted to dealing exclusively or mainly with the type of disputes[15] specified in the service contracts. There might then be problems guaranteeing equal access for all potential users of the service, particularly where the 'service level agreement' represents the sole or main source of funding for the service.

The former model has the advantage of preserving a greater degree of independence for the service, but the funds might not be sufficient to enable mediators to be paid, or even to deal with the number of cases referred.

The issue of paid versus volunteer mediators is one for those providing mediation services to address, but we suspect that if the service is to move towards an increasing reliance on professional mediators, the likeliest way of securing funding for this would involve an increasing reliance on service contracts negotiated with local authorities.

Promoting the use of mediation

Even where mediation services are already in existence, however, they appear to be relatively under-utilised by local authorities, and as many as three quarters of all mediation services indicated that they would like to receive more referrals. One problem is felt to be that some potential referrers are not sufficiently aware of the service or its potential benefits. One respondent to our housing survey questionnaire also spoke of the difficulty involved in establishing a culture within the department that is more supportive of mediation. This is also an important policy issue confronting the service, and it may be that closer collaboration between mediators and local authority housing and environmental health officials over the issue of referral criteria could help to address the problem.

Another practice that might help to bring about an increase in the level of referrals while at the same time enabling referrers to identify the most suitable cases for referral would be to provide more detailed feed-back of the outcomes reached in those cases that are referred. Housing officials in Council B, while supportive of mediation in principle, complained that they were not kept informed of the progress of cases they referred for mediation.

Finally, another factor that helps to account for the relatively modest use of mediation even in areas where it is available, is that many disputants in potentially mediatable cases do not wish to participate in the process. It would not be in keeping with the ethos of the service to force disputants to take part in mediation, but it may be that more could be done to promote the approach and overcome resistance to it. For example, tenants' handbooks could include a section on dealing with neighbour disputes, and might usefully draw attention to the limitations associated with traditional ways of dealing with the problem.

Suggestions for further research

As is often the case with research of this kind, we have found that by probing the issues we have simply established how little we know about the problem, and how much more is still to be done. We therefore conclude the report by briefly identifying some further topics for research in the field of neighbour disputes:

- to identify the resource costs involved (and potential for savings to be made by diverting appropriate cases to mediation) in respect of other agencies, viz. police, courts (including legal aid fund), solicitors, citizens' advice bureaux, health service, local authority social service departments and legal and administration departments.

- to undertake a comparative consumer satisfaction survey to elicit the views and perceptions of a sample of disputants whose disputes have been handled by means of a) mediation; and b) conventional approaches.

- to explore (possibly in conjunction with the above study) the scope for using perceptual indicators relating to the quality of life (of the kind that have been developed by Glasgow University's Applied Population Research Unit) as a way of measuring non-monetary outcomes associated with the different ways of dealing with neighbour disputes.

- to develop and seek to operationalise the kind of typology we propose on page 87 in order to ascertain the proportion of cases within a sample of housing areas that might be amenable to mediation and to refine a set of referral criteria based on this approach.

- To seek to establish more of the direct salary and non-salary costs (e.g. care-takers, direct works, allocations and homeless section housing staff plus the cost of repairs and refurbishment) incurred by housing departments as a result of neighbour disputes. As we explained in the report, such an exercise would require a much greater degree of collaboration with housing staff than was required even for the current project.

Notes

1 The numbers in brackets following each category refer to the case histories we have examined in the report and which might serve to illustrate the different categories to which we refer.

2 As we have seen, neighbour disputes tend not to be identified as a separate category at all, let alone according to the issues involved.

3 In theory housing allocations staff can have a very important and valuable preventive role in trying to avoid assigning families or individuals that are likely to prove incompatible with one another, but in practice their room for manoeuvre is likely to be seriously limited by the (non-) availability of suitable accommodation.

4 Caution is needed, since there are fears that this could result in a two-tier justice system in which the poor would be denied access to the courts. However, it is worth noting that in the United States the biggest users of private alternative dispute resolution services are in fact major corporations involved in highly complex and expensive lawsuits, and for whom expense is not a problem (Menkel-Meadow, 1996: 98).

5 It might also be appropriate to consider whether it might be a more productive use of legal aid funds to pay for the services of an accredited mediator in such cases as an alternative to expensive and often futile legal action.

6 Thus obviating the need for (and expense of) rehousing, which is what happened in this particular case.

7 We did come across one case involving serious and prolonged racial harassment in which a novel attempt was made by the mediation service in Sheffield (MESH) to undertake a form of 'community mediation' involving a whole street. Although the approach did not succeed on this occasion (mainly because of a reluctance on the part of several of the parties to participate), there may be circumstances where mediation could have a part to play in seeking to resolve such issues. It is also worth noting that among victim offender mediation schemes, the one at Leeds does attempt to work even with very serious offenders, who may have been tried and punished in the normal way; for example, where the victim might have an interest in confronting the offender and the latter is prepared to go along with this.

8 Not least of these is the danger of 'ghettoisation'

9 Ideally this would be devised in consultation with mediation services at either local or national level and might consist of an explanatory leaflet advocating a problem-solving approach to neighbour problems and outlining the extent (and limitations) of existing powers and remedies, together with information about the use of alternative remedies such as mediation. Complainants could be advised to return to the department if the problem persists, but might be warned that the council would normally expect parties to have attempted to resolve their differences informally before becoming involved in the matter.

10 Another advantage would be that the pack could be issued in response to all enquiries, irrespective of any restrictions on the categories of complainants who are deemed eligible to receive assistance from the housing department.

11 One felt that 40% of cases could be categorised at the outset or soon after the complaint has been lodged.

12 We do not ourselves favour their use for reasons which we summarise in the following paragraph.

13 See Figure 4.9 above, on page 29.

14 Mainly from central government in the case of victim support.

15 Or parties; for example those renting their housing from the local authority.

References

Acland, A.F. (1995), 'Simply negotiation with knobs on', *Legal Action*, November 1995, pp: 10-15.

Aldbourne Associates, (1993), *Managing Neighbour Complaints in Social Housing: A Handbook for Practitioners*, Aldbourne: Aldbourne Associates.

Building Research Establishment (BRE) (1993), Effects of Environmental Noise on People at Home: BRE Information Paper 22/93. Construction Research Communication Ltd.

Bush, R.A. Baruch and Folger, J.P. (1994), *The Promise of Mediation: Responding to Conflict Through Empowerment and Recognition*, San Francisco: Jossey-Bass.

Cornwell, P. (1995), 'Good neighbours policy', *Guardian 'Society'*, 17 May 1995

Davis, G., Boucherat, J. and Watson, D. (1987), *A preliminary study of victim offender mediation and reparation schemes in England and Wales*. Research and Planning Unit Paper 42. London: HMSO.

Department of the Environment (1995), *Review of the Effectiveness of Neighbour Noise Controls*

Department of the Environment (1996), *Digest of Environmental Statistics*, No. 18. London: HMSO.

Dignan, J. and Sorsby, A. (1995), *Towards a National Database for Mediation Services* (unpublished).

Dignan, J. Sorsby, A. and Hibbert, J. (1996), *Neighbour Dispute Mediation: Public Agencies General Survey* (unpublished).

General Accident (1995), *Good Neighbours Survey*. Unpublished report.

Karn, V., Lickiss, R., Hughes, D. and Crawley, J. (1993), *Neighbour Disputes: Responses by Social Landlords*. Coventry: Institute of Housing.

Kemp, C., Norris, C. and Fielding, N.G. (1992), *Negotiating Nothing: Police Decision-making in Disputes*, Aldershot: Avebury.

Madge, N. (1996), 'Housing Act, 1996', *Legal Action*, October 1996, pp: 10-15.

Marshall, T. and Walpole, M. (1985), *Bringing People Together: Mediation and Reparation Projects in Great Britain*. Research and Planning Unit Paper 33. London: HMSO.

Mediation UK (1993), *Guide to starting a Community Mediation Service*. Bristol: Mediation UK.

Mediation UK (1996), *Mediation Digest*, no. 3

Menkel-Meadow, C. (1996), 'Will managed care give us access to justice?' in Roger Smith, *Achieving Civil Justice: Appropriate Dispute Resolution for the 1990s*, London: Legal Action Group.

Safe Neighbourhoods Unit (1993), *Crime Prevention on Council Estates*. London: HMSO.

Woolf, Lord (1995), *Access to Justice* (Woolf Inquiry Team, 1995).

Appendices

Appendix 1: Criteria considered in accepting case

Service	Criteria
Worthing	Geographical. New organisation, still feeling way
Whitstable	At least willingness for letter approach to 2nd party No other option already chosen e.g. moving leaving little time Conditional on process of any offence & court settlement No win/ lose strongly held No wish to use as 'judging' messenger Ability to operate even handedly
Maidstone	Willingness of first party to participate
Plymouth	Both parties agree to mediation
Cambridge	Acceptance of principles of mediation by first party
Lambeth	Difficult cases are discussed
Derby	Geographical, though will offer office visit to cases outside Derby
Wandsworth	Willingness of both/all parties to meet and mediate
Bromley	Whether client wishes to proceed when mode of activity of service fully explained
Bolton	Cannot work with: people for whom it is extremely difficult to communicate, negotiate, or to sustain the level of communication required for the negotiation process; people known to be involved in criminal activity; people known to be violent; people currently taking legal action against their neighbours (this does not include police involvement); large groups of children. Can mediate with: children; people who have been involved in legal action; those referred by police; some people with learning disabilities; those for whom English is not their first language; older people; deaf people
Sandwell	Both parties willing and Sandwell residents.
Mid Wales	Policy still being developed current guidelines: I) Is neighbour dispute (rather than couple/ family) 2) Not been presented to courts for adjudication 3) Not large sums of money/ capital being disputed 4) is agreement as to who parties are
Brighton	Have accepted all cases so far
Tallaght	Are prepared to sit down in a joint face to face session to negotiate the issues
Dorset	Willingness of both parties to accept mediation and conditions
Luton	Willingness to use a non-punitive method

Service	Criteria
Coventry	Won't accept case with known history of threatening behaviour
Bideford	Geographical, nature of dispute./ situation
Camden	In development. Considerations include: mental health issues/ violence/ serious harassment; other current action; length of case; willingness and ability to resolve; substance abuse; neighbour dispute or other type of case
Lewisham	Don't accept cases concerning: people with mental health problems; alcoholics; racial abuse
Sheffield	Geographical; willingness of parties to accept their involvement; involves neighbours or near resident; degree of violence involved; whether involves racial harassment; whether is serious power imbalance; whether psychotic mental illness is factor
Bilston	Is a neighbour dispute and both parties willing for their involvement; don't accept cases involving racism or with court proceedings in progress
Oxford	Is service appropriate and likely to reduce/ resolve conflict
Dundee	Not yet operational
Edinburgh	Not yet operational. In process of formulating criteria
Bristol	Geographical; willingness of client; may have to turn away cases when totally overloaded
Newham	Whether case suitable for mediation; whether parties willing to mediate; whether have resources (mediators, conciliators, venue and time) to match the particular case and parties background and personal details
Milton Keynes	Geographical; neighbour dispute; appropriate to service; legal implications; risk of violence
Unite	Both parties understand what mediation is and are willing to take part; situation not dangerous to mediators
Southwark	At least one party must live in Borough of Southwark; first party must express willingness to take part in mediation and give permission for them to contact second party
Leeds	Power balance/imbalance; willingness of party making contact to give it a go

Appendix 2a: Council A Area [a] Costs

Costs Per Hour and Per Case Based on Actual Case Records

Salary Analysis / Total Costs and Hours	No of Posts	Salary only £	Costs Full Costs £	Full Direct £	Hours per Annum Total Hours	Neighbour Nuisance Prop'n *	Neighbour Nuisance Hours	Total Hours Cost Rates per Hour Salary only £	Full Costs £	Average Hrs per Case	Av. Costs per Case Salary only £	Full Costs £
Area Manager	1	25,636	47,271	NA	1,762.50	—	—	14.55	NA	—	—	NA
Asst Area Manager	1	21,339	39,348	NA	1,762.50	—	—	12.11	NA	—	—	NA
Senior Mgt Officer	2	31,436	57,966	144,585	3,525.00	0.00	3.24	8.92	41.02	0.03	0.25	1.14
Mgt Officer	7	99,617	183,687	347,547	12,337.50	0.02	199.90	8.07	28.17	1.71	13.80	48.13
Clerk/WPO	8	88,864	163,860	NA	14,100.00	—	—	6.30	NA	—	—	NA
		266,892	492,132	492,132	33,487.50	0.00	203.14		14.70	1.74	14.04	49.27
Other staff (caretakers, benefits team)		274,958	507,005									
		541,850	999,137									

* From case hours as a proportion of total hours

Costs Per Hour and Per Case Based on Time Records

Salary Analysis / Total Costs and Hours	No of Posts	Salary only £	Costs Full Costs £	Full Direct £	Hours per Annum Total Hours	Neighbour Nuisance Prop'n *	Neighbour Nuisance Hours	Total Hours Cost Rates per Hour Salary only £	Full Costs £	Average Hrs per Case	Av. Costs per Case Salary only £	Full Costs £
Area Manager	1	25,636	47,271		1,762.50	0.07	119.85	14.55	26.82	1.02	14.90	27.47
Asst Area Manager	1	21,339	39,348		1,762.50	0.07	119.85	12.11	22.32	1.02	12.40	22.87
Senior Mgt Officer	2	31,436	57,966		3,525.00	0.08	297.86	8.92	16.44	2.55	22.70	41.86
Mgt Officer	7	99,617	183,687		12,337.50	0.08	1,042.52	8.07	14.89	8.91	71.95	132.66
Clerk/WPO	8	88,864	163,860		14,100.00	0.01	204.45	6.30	11.62	1.75	11.01	20.31
		266,892	492,132	492,132	33,487.50		1,784.53		14.70	15.25	132.96	245.18
Other staff (caretakers, benefits team)		274,958	507,005									
		541,850	999,137									

* From internal "Results of time monitoring" exercise carried out in two housing area offices during 4 weeks of June 1994.
NB Area (a) not one of those reported on.

Appendix 2b: Council A Area [a]

Case Cost Analysis by Outcome Activity [Using Full Cost Rates]

	Case Cost £	Cost per Case by Outcome (*)							
		0 £	1 £	2 £	3 £	4 £	5 £	6 £	7 £
Total Cost	5764.10	367.24	2440.63	954.86	12.56	0.00	998.73	975.22	14.85
No in Outcome Category	117	7	60	11	1	0	16	21	1
Average Cost of Outcome Category	49.27	52.46	40.68	86.81	12.56	0.00	62.42	46.44	14.85
Range of Cost — Minimum	7.04	9.39	8.66	10.16	12.56	0.00	9.39	7.04	14.85
Maximum	276.16	140.85	117.25	276.16	12.56	0.00	184.69	94.73	14.85

	Outcome Code
*	Outcome Code
0	Unknown
1	Doesn't recur
2	Alleged perpetrator moved
3	Resolved without intervention
4	Other
5	Complainant moves
6	Problem recurs
7	Recurs with different neighbour

Case Cost Analysis by Type of Move [Using Full Cost Rates]

	Case Cost £	Cost per Case by Outcome (*)					
		0 £	1 £	2 £	3 £	4 £	5 £
Total Cost	1713.07	185.03	40.08	0.00	232.62	960.69	294.64
No in Outcome Category	24	2	1	0	3	12	6
Average Cost of Outcome Category	71.38	92.52	40.08	0.00	77.54	80.06	49.11
Range of Cost — Minimum	9.39	19.65	40.08	0.00	19.76	10.16	9.39
Maximum	276.16	165.38	40.08	0.00	184.69	276.16	169.02

	Outcome Code
*	Outcome Code
0	Unknown
1	Abandonment
2	NA
3	Notice given by tenant
4	Transferred
5	Mutual Exchange

Appendix 3: Council A Area (b) – Case 12

Dates	Time Mins	Event Type	Cum Time Mins	Staff Grade	Time Hours	Proportion of Staff Grade Time AM %	AAM %	SMO %	MO %	Cost of Staff Time by Event AM £	AAM £	SMO £	MO £	Total £	Cum Time Hrs	Cum Cost £
06-Jun-95	60	Letter in	60	MO	1.00				100%				14.36	14.36	1.00	14.36
22-Jun-95	30	Office mtg	90	MO	0.50				100%				7.18	7.18	1.50	21.55
19-Jul-95	40	Office mtg	130	MO	0.67				100%				9.58	9.58	2.17	31.12
18-Aug-95	60	NSP issued	190	MO	1.00				100%				14.36	14.36	3.17	45.48
21-Aug-95	40	Office mtg	230	MO	0.67				100%				9.58	9.58	3.83	55.06
30-Aug-95	20	Phone in	250	MO	0.33				100%				4.79	4.79	4.17	59.85
18-Sep-95	15	Phone in	265	MO	0.25				100%				3.59	3.59	4.42	63.44
21-Dec-95	40	Office mtg	305	MO	0.67				100%				9.58	9.58	5.08	73.01
11-Jan-96	20	Letter in	325	MO	0.33				100%				4.79	4.79	5.42	77.80
11-Jan-96	60	Visit	385	MO	1.00				100%				14.36	14.36	6.42	92.17
18-Jan-96	40	Visit	425	MO	0.67				100%				9.58	9.58	7.08	101.74
19-Feb-96	40	Office mtg	465	MO	0.67				100%				9.58	9.58	7.75	111.32
26-Feb-96	80	Letter out	545	MO	1.33				100%				19.15	19.15	9.08	130.47
07-Mar-96	15	Letter in	560	MO	0.25				100%				3.59	3.59	9.33	134.06
09-Mar-96	10	Letter in	570	MO	0.17				100%				2.39	2.39	9.50	136.45
11-Mar-96	60	Letter in	630	MO	1.00				100%				14.36	14.36	10.50	150.82
29-Mar-96	30	Letter in	660	MO	0.50				100%				7.18	7.18	11.00	158.00
04-Apr-96	10	Letter in	670	MO	0.17				100%				2.39	2.39	11.17	160.39
07-Apr-96	0	Letter in	670	MO	—				100%				—	—	11.17	160.39
08-Apr-96	10	Letter in	680	AM	0.17	100%				4.31				4.31	11.33	164.71
10-Apr-96	10	Letter in	690	SMO	0.17			100%				2.64		2.64	11.50	167.35
10-Apr-96	15	Letter in	705	MO	0.25				100%				3.59	3.59	11.75	170.94
10-Apr-96	60	Draft NSP	765	SMO	1.00			100%				15.86		15.86	12.75	186.80
11-Apr-96	0	Letter in	765	MO	—				100%				—	—	12.75	186.80
11-Apr-96	5	Draft NSP	770	SMO	0.08			100%				1.32		1.32	12.83	188.13
11-Apr-96	90	Office mtg & letter out	860	MO	1.50				100%				21.55	21.55	14.33	209.67
Total	**860**				**14.33**					**4.31**	**—**	**19.83**	**185.53**	**209.67**		

Elapsed Time of Process: 0.85 Years

Key to Staff Grade

AM	Area Manager	SMO	Senior Management Officer
AAM	Assistant Area Manager	MO	Management Officer

Appendix 4: Council A Environmental Health Department Costs

Costs Per Hour and Per Case Based on Actual Case Records

Salary Analysis	No of Posts	Costs		Total Hours	Neighbour Nuisance Prop'n *	Neighbour Nuisance Hours	Hours per Annum	Cost Rates per Hour			Total Hours	Study		Average Costs per Case		
		Salary only £	Full Costs £				Salary only £	Full Costs £	Internal £		Salary only £	Full Costs £	Average Hrs per Case	Salary only £	Full Costs £
Total Costs and Hours																
Area Manager	1	30,000	37,408	1,533	1	1533	19.57	24.40	22.62						
Principal Officer	1	26,045	32,477	1,533	1	1533	16.99	21.18	20.04						
EH Officer	9	209,187	260,844	13,797	1	13797	15.16	18.91	18.21		21.20	26.44	0.22	4.71	5.87
EH Technician	24	426,504	531,825	36,792	1	36792	11.59	14.45	14.64		12.65	15.78	0.22	2.81	3.50
Dog Warden	4	53,308	66,472	6,132	1	6132	8.69	10.84	11.74						
Manual Worker	1	13,000	16,210	1,533	1	1533	8.48	10.57	15.45						
Office Manager	1	19,000	23,692	1,533	1	1533	12.39	15.45	11.53						
Receptionists	6	54,762	68,285	9,198	1	9198	5.95	7.42	9.00		8.02	10.00	0.27	2.15	2.68
		831,806	1,037,213	72,051		72051	11.54	14.40						9.67	12.06

* Using a flat £3.05 per head

Appendix 5a: Sandwell Data Summary

Case Event Type	Amended Average Event Hrs	Form C Average Hours	Average from event analysis	Employee Grade Involved	Time Proportions by Staff Grade				Calculated Hours of Staff Grade Times				
					PA	PM	PC	VM	PA	PM	PC	VM	Total
Travel Time	1.92			PM		1.00				1.58			1.58
Postage													
Other Expenses													
Calls In (No)													
Calls In (Time)	0.21	0.00	0.11	PA/PM/PC	0.33	0.33	0.33		0.06	0.06	0.06		0.17
Calls Out (No)													
Calls Out (Time)	0.31	0.25	0.11	PA/PM/PC	0.33	0.33	0.33		0.05	0.05	0.05		0.16
Letters In (No)													
Letters Out (No)													
Letters Out (Time)	0.16	0.25		PA	1.00				0.11				0.11
Home Visits (No)													
Home Visits(Time)	2.84	2.00	1.11	PM/PC		0.50	0.50			1.14	1.14		2.28
Office Visits (No)													
Office Visits(Time)	0.94	1.00	0.69	PM/PC		0.50	0.50			0.06	0.06		0.12
Other Visits (No)													
Other Visits (Time)	12.62	3.00	0.38	PM/PC		0.50	0.50			0.83	0.83		1.66
TOTALS	19.00	6.50	2.39										
Case administration activities													
Recording referral	0.05	0.05	0.05	PA/PM/PC	0.33	0.33	0.33		0.02	0.02	0.02		0.05
Liaising with referring organisation	0.25	0.25	0.25	PM/PC		0.50	0.50			0.13	0.13		0.25
Investigating the circumstances	1.00	1.00	1.00	PM/PC		0.50	0.50			0.50	0.50		1.00
Addressing suitability of case	0.25	0.25	0.25	PM/PC		0.50	0.50			0.13	0.13		0.25
Recording outcome of mediation	0.33	0.33	0.33	PM/PC/VM		0.33	0.33	0.33		0.11	0.11	0.11	0.33
Keeping statistics,filling in forms,etc.	0.25	0.25	0.25	PM/PC/VM		0.33	0.33	0.33		0.08	0.08	0.08	0.25
Conducting follow-up survey	0.17	0.17	0.17	PA/PM/PC	0.33	0.33	0.33		0.06	0.06	0.06		0.17
Preparation activities	2.00	2.00	2.00	PA/PM/PC/VM	0.25	0.25	0.25	0.25	0.50	0.50	0.50	0.50	2.00
TOTALS	23.30	10.80	6.69						0.79	5.23	3.66	0.69	10.37

Appendix 5b: Sandwell Timesheet Analysis

Four weeks ending 15th October 1995: All Hours Expended

		Co-Ordinator		Administrator		Mediator	
		Hrs	%	Hrs	%	Hrs	%
Victim/Offender	Direct	4.67		4.00		21.58	
	Indirect Prop'n	12.60					
Total		17.27	14.44%	4.00	19.75%	21.58	17.75%
Neighbourhood	Direct	27.67		16.25		100.00	
	Indirect Prop'n	74.63					
Total		102.30	85.56%	16.25	80.25%	100.00	82.25%
Indirect		87.23		51.25		0.00	
Apportionment:							
Victim/Offender		12.60		10.12		0.00	
Neighbourhood		74.63		41.13		0.00	

Total Time Breakdown	Co-Ordinator		Administrator		Mediator	
	Hrs	%	Hrs	%	Hrs	%
Victim/Offender	4.67	4%	4.00	6%	21.58	18%
Neighbourhood	27.67	23%	16.25	23%	100.00	82%
Indirect	87.23	73%	51.25	72%	0.00	0%
	119.57	100%	71.50	100%	121.58	100%

All Hours Expended Excluding PR, Fund Raising, Consultancy and VSS work

		Co-Ordinator		Administrator		Mediator	
		Hrs	%	Hrs	%	Hrs	%
Victim/Offender	Direct	4.67		4.00		21.58	
	Indirect Prop'n	10.74					
Total		15.41	14.44%	4.00	19.75%	21.58	17.75%
Neighbourhood	Direct	27.67		16.25		100.00	
	Indirect Prop'n	63.66					
Total		91.33	85.56%	16.25	80.25%	100.00	82.25%
Indirect		74.4		38.25		0.00	
Apportionment:							
Victim/Offender		10.74		7.56		0.00	
Neighbourhood		63.66		30.69		0.00	

Total Time Breakdown	Co-Ordinator		Administrator		Mediator	
	Hrs	%	Hrs	%	Hrs	%
Victim/Offender	4.67	4%	4.00	6%	21.58	18%
Neighbourhood	27.67	23%	16.25	23%	100.00	82%
Indirect	74.4	62%	38.25	53%	0.00	0%
	106.74	89%	58.50	82%	121.58	100%

Appendix 5c: Sandwell CMS: Costings Based on Timesheet Data for the Four Weeks Ended 15th October 1995

Salary Analysis	Costs Salary only £	Full Costs £	Hours per Annum Total	Indirect	Direct	Total Hours Cost Rates per Hour Salary only £	Full Costs £	Direct Hours Cost Rates per Hour Salary only £	Full Costs £	Average Hrs per Case	Average Costs per Case Salary only £	Full Costs £
Total Costs and Hours												
Co-ordinator	16,470	21,918	1645	1200	445	10.01	13.32	37.02	49.26	3.66	135.36	180.14
Administrator	8,583	11,422	1410	1011	399	6.09	8.10	21.49	28.60	0.79	16.94	22.54
Mediators	13,775	18,332	2209	0	2209	6.24	8.30	6.24	8.30	5.93	36.96	49.18
Total	38,828	51,672	5264	2211	3053					10.37	189.26	251.86
Victim/Offender Costs and Hours												
Co-ordinator	2,378	3,165	64		64							
Administrator	1,695	2,256	79		79							
Mediators	2,445	3,254	392		392							
Total	6,519	8,675			535							
Neighbourhood Costs and Hours												
Co-ordinator	14,092	18,753			381							
Administrator	6,888	9,166			320							
Mediators	11,330	15,078			1817							
Total	32,309	42,997			2518							

Cases per year Capability		No
Cases per Year (@ Full Cost per Case)	104	171
Cases per Year (Actual 1994/95)	407	137
Potential for Case Load increase %	307	20%
	171	

[Excluding Indirect Time for PR, Fund Raising, Consultancy and VSS Work]

Salary Analysis	Costs Salary only £	Full Costs £	Hours per Annum Total	Indirect	Direct	Total Hours Cost Rates per Hour Salary only £	Full Costs £	Direct Hours Cost Rates per Hour Salary only £	Full Costs £	Average Hrs per Case	Average Costs per Case Salary only £	Full Costs £
Total Costs and Hours												
Co-ordinator	16,470	21,918	1645	1024	621	10.01	13.32	26.50	35.27	3.66	96.91	128.97
Administrator	8,583	11,422	1410	754	656	6.09	8.10	13.09	17.42	0.79	10.32	13.73
Mediators	13,775	18,332	2209	0	2209	6.24	8.30	6.24	8.30	5.93	36.96	49.18
Total	38,828	51,672	5264	1778	3486					10.37	144.19	191.88
Victim/Offender Costs and Hours												
Co-ordinator	2,378	3,165	90		90							
Administrator	1,695	2,256	130		130							
Mediators	2,445	3,254	392		392							
Total	6,519	8,675			611							
Neighbourhood Costs and Hours												
Co-ordinator	14,092	18,753			532							
Administrator	6,888	9,166			526							
Mediators	11,330	15,078			1817							
Total	32,309	42,997			2875							

Cases per year Capability		No
Cases per Year (@ Full Cost per Case)	145	224
Cases per Year (Actual 1994/95)	668	137
307 Potential for Case Load increase %	39%	
	224	

Appendix 5d: Sandwell CMS: Analysis of Times and Cost per Case by Stage

Staff Grade Cost per Hour			
PA £	PM £	PC £	VM £
28.60	8.30	49.26	8.30

	Average Number per Case	Calculated Hours of Staff Grade Times						Average Costs of Staff Grade Times					
		PA Hrs	PM Hrs	PC Hrs	VM Hrs	Total Hrs	Cum Hrs	PA £	PM £	PC £	VM £	Total £	Cumm £
Recording referral	1	0.02	0.02	0.02		0.05	0.05	0.48	0.14	0.82		1.44	1.44
Liaising with referring organisation	1		0.13	0.13		0.25	0.30		1.04	6.16		7.20	8.63
Investigating the circumstances	1		0.50	0.50		1.00	1.30		4.15	24.63		28.78	37.41
Addressing suitability of case	1		0.13	0.13		0.25	1.55		1.04	6.16		7.20	44.61
Calls In	1.46	0.06	0.06	0.06		0.17	1.72	1.62	0.47	2.79		4.88	49.48
Calls Out	1.16	0.05	0.05	0.05		0.16	1.88	1.55	0.45	2.67		4.66	54.15
Letters out	1.21	0.11				0.11	1.82	3.01				3.01	57.16
Preparation activities	?	0.50	0.50	0.50	0.50	2.00	3.88	14.30	4.15	24.63	4.15	47.23	104.39
Home Visits	1.87		1.14	1.14		2.28	6.16		9.46	56.17		65.63	170.02
Mileage			1.58			1.58	7.74		13.07			13.07	183.09
Office Visits	0.16		0.06	0.06		0.12	7.86		0.51	3.03		3.54	186.63
Other Visits	1.11		0.83	0.83		1.66	9.52		6.87	40.77		47.64	234.27
Recording outcome of mediation	1		0.11	0.11	0.11	0.33	9.85		0.92	5.47	0.92	7.32	241.59
Keeping statistics, filling in forms, etc.	1		0.08	0.08	0.08	0.25	10.10		0.69	4.11	0.69	5.49	247.08
Conducting follow-up survey	1	0.06	0.06	0.06		0.17	10.27	1.59	0.46	2.74		4.79	251.86
		0.79	5.23	3.66	0.69	10.37		22.54	43.42	180.14	5.76	251.86	

Appendix 5e: Sandwell CMS: Case Cost Analysis by Outcome Activity [Using Full Cost Rates]

	Case Cost £	Cost per Case by Outcome (*)				
		0 £	1 £	2 £	3 £	4 £
Total Cost	15180.05	302.78	828.60	2192.86	4748.28	7107.54
No in Outcome Category	61	2	7	14	15	23
Average Cost of Outcome Category	248.85	151.39	118.37	156.63	316.55	309.02
Range of Cost — Minimum		150.92	109.43	109.43	146.80	191.92
Maximum		151.85	133.37	216.01	1090.62	890.03

* Outcome Code
0 Not recorded
1 Letters/phone calls
2 Advice/support one party, no attempt to contact other
3 Advice/support one party, attempt to contact other
4 Work with two or more parties

Appendix 6: Derby Community Mediation Service

Costings based on estimates made using Form C and reported weekly working hours by grade for a 9 month period

Salary Analysis	Costs Salary only £	Costs Full Costs £	Hours per Annum Total	Indirect	Direct	Total Hours Cost Rates per Hour Salary only £	Full Costs £	Direct Hours* Cost Rates per Hour Salary only £	Full Costs £	Average Hrs per Case	Average Costs per Case Salary only £	Full Costs £
Total Costs and Hours												
Co-ordinator	12,061	—	1,321	1,321	—	9.13	0.00	9.13	0.00			
Admin Assistant												
Mediators	—	31,194	4,230	846	3,384	0.00	7.37	3.56	9.22	8.80	31.36	81.11
Total	12,061	31,194	5,551	2,167	3,384	9.13	7.37	3.56	9.22	8.80	31.36	81.11

* Total costs divided by mediator hours

Victim/Offender & Workmen Costs and Hours

	Costs Salary only £	Full Costs £	Total	Indirect	Direct
Co-ordinator	—	—	—		
Admin Assistant	—	—			
Mediators	936	102	102	102	—
Total	936	102	102	102	

Neighbourhood Costs and Hours

	Costs Salary only £	Full Costs £	Total	Indirect	Direct
Co-ordinator	12,061	—			
Admin Assistant	—	—			
Mediators	—	30,258	3,282		3,282
Total	12,061	30,258	3,282		3,282

Cases per year Capability	No
Co-ordinator	NA
Admin Assistant	NA
Mediators	373
Cases per Year (@ Full Cost per Case)	385
Cases per Year (Actual 1994/95)	162
Potential for Case Load increase %	58%

1. Clearly, with all direct work being done by volunteer mediators, the actual cost per case is the overall costs of the service divided by the hours spent on cases by the volunteer mediators.

Costings based on the table above but with an imputed cost for volunteer time added.

Salary Analysis	Costs Salary only £	Costs Full Costs £	Hours per Annum Total	Indirect	Direct	Total Hours Cost Rates per Hour Salary only £	Full Costs £	Direct Hours* Cost Rates per Hour Salary only £	Full Costs £	Average Hrs per Case	Average Costs per Case Salary only £	Full Costs £
Total Costs and Hours												
Co-ordinator	12,061	—	1,321	1,321	—	9.13	0.00	9.13	0.00			
Admin Assistant												
Mediators	31,217	62,411	4,230	846	3,384	7.38	14.75	9.23	18.44	8.80	81.17	162.29
Total	43,278	62,411	5,551	2,167	3,384	16.51	14.75	9.23	18.44	8.80	81.17	162.29

* Total costs divided by mediator hours

Victim/Offender & Workmen Costs and Hours

	Costs Salary only £	Full Costs £	Total	Indirect	Direct
Co-ordinator	—	—	—		
Admin Assistant	—	—			
Mediators	937	1,872	102	102	—
Total	937	1,872	102	102	

Neighbourhood Costs and Hours

	Costs Salary only £	Full Costs £	Total	Indirect	Direct
Co-ordinator	12,061	62,411			
Admin Assistant	—	—			
Mediators	30,281	60,539	3,282		3,282
Total	42,342	122,950	3,282		3,282

Cases per year Capability	No
Co-ordinator	NA
Admin Assistant	NA
Mediators	373
Cases per Year (@ Full Cost per Case)	522
Cases per Year (Actual 1994/95)	162
Potential for Case Load increase %	69%

1. We have assumed an hourly rate for the volunteers of £7.38 per hour (April 1993 New Earnings Survey).
2. Because the co-ordinator is doing PR and fund raising work her time is a straight on-cost and we have added the full cost of her employment to the implied cost of the volunteer mediators to arrive at the cost per hour and per case.

UNIVERSITY / URC / SET (library stamp)